Praise for

FOUR MONTHS ... AND A LIFETIME

"Chris has written a touching story of a father and his son playing, coaching, and falling in love with the greatest game on earth. It is both captivating and filled with great anecdotes from a guy who truly knows and loves the game."

—Brian "White Mamba" Scalabrine, Boston Celtics, Chicago Bulls, and New Jersey Nets

"Touching, uplifting, inspirational and a heck of a lot of fun."

—Gregory Zuckerman, co-author of *Rising Above: How 11 Athletes Overcame Challenges in Their Youth to Become Stars, The Man Who Solved the Market,* and *The Frackers*

"Chris Meyer has penned a family basketball odyssey—a journey from the hardwood court to the heart of a father/son relationship. His deftly balanced prose has the feel of a basketball resting comfortably on your fingertips."

—Paul Volponi, author of *Black and White, The Final Four,* and *Streetball is Life*

"Unsuspecting readers might think they've simply picked up a primer on the joys and pitfalls of coaching middle school basketball. But Chris Meyer's meticulously crafted work intertwines his deep love of family with an expansive knowledge of basketball, especially the nuanced ways in which the game can foster teamwork and reveal the true character of those who are caught up in its orbit. Of particular interest is the author's endearing description of what it's like to call "next" as a newcomer in a seemingly hostile gym, which reads like a youthful but not necessarily naïve hostage negotiator rescuing a long-lost family heirloom from a grumpy pawnbroker."

—Craig Leener, author of *This Was Never About Basketball* and *All Roads Lead to Lawrence*

OTHER BOOKS BY CHRIS MEYER:

*Life in 20 Lessons: What a Funeral Guy
Discovered About Life, From Death*

The 'Wood

The Book of Moments
(coming in 2022)

FOUR MONTHS

...AND A LIFETIME

A Father, His Son, and Their Epic
Basketball Team's Nine-Year Journey Together

CHRIS MEYER

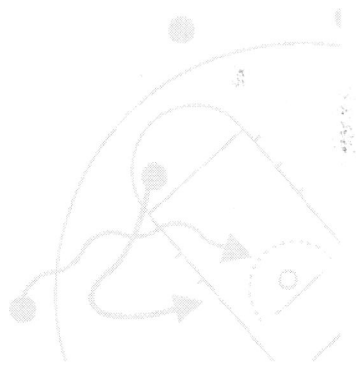

Four Months ... and a Lifetime
Copyright © 2020 Chris Meyer

ISBN (print, soft cover): 978-1-7333443-5-7
ISBN (print, hard cover): 978-1-7333443-4-0
ISBN (ebook): 978-1-7333443-6-4
ISBN (audiobook): 978-1-7333443-7-1

Editorial: Sandra Wendel, Write On, Inc.
Design: Domini Dragoone
Cover and interior images: Marcin Jucha/123rf, Ñitin Řana/Pexels,
    Augustas Cetkauskas/iStock

Published by:
Meaning of Life Publishing
chrismeyerauthor.com

The game has been good.
—VINCE CARTER

Thank you for coaching
my basketball team, Dad.
—BROCK MEYER

CONTENTS

INTRODUCTION

Coaches, coaches of all sports.

This is for you.

We are all so different. We all have different styles and approaches. But we all choose to coach children. We, hopefully, choose to impact the lives of these boys and girls to instill in them the joy of the game. To show them how sport is a microcosm of the life that will confront them all too soon.

How exciting it is to work together toward a common goal with your friends, or people with whom you share a common interest but may otherwise have very little in common with or, previously, may have never even met. It is truly a wonderful experience. An experience for life and the manifold jobs these kids will all surely have.

Winning.

Yes, we are all hell-bent on winning. Somehow this is always the litmus test of society. This is the ugly part of the game. I am no different, and, in many ways, I am far worse. I have been there. I have pushed too hard and cared too much about winning. Usually my wife, my son, or a friend will remind me that it is just a game.

They are always right.

All my life, I have instinctively revered coaches, yet my father never even coached me once. Instead, he worked tirelessly to provide for his family. Sports were simply not his thing (the irony of all ironies). I knew very early on in my life that coaches were men who were giving of their time. Men who came from work, often in their work clothes, and who quickly changed in their car and tried to teach us the fundamentals and strategies of the game for those few short hours a week.

I always respected them.

I am not even certain it was because my parents told me to respect them, I just innately knew these men deserved my respect. I could see that they coached for the love of the game and to be with their sons and whichever friends the recreation league gave them to coach that year.

And I came ready. I was always there ready to be taught.

A coach has a profound impact on a child's life.

I know.

I was one of those kids.

I know.

I hope to be one of those coaches too.

LOCKED AND LOADED

The rim is 18 inches wide.

When properly inflated to a pressure of 7.5 to 8.5 pounds per square inch, a 29.5-inch basketball has a diameter ranging from 9.43 to 9.51 inches. Its maximum weight is 22 ounces. The object of the game is to get that ball inside of that rim—or prevent it from happening if you are playing defense.

The game is so simple.

And that ball. Its feel to my touch. The almost religious-like quality of the full grain leather in my hand. The indented black lines undulating to the raised, scale-like dimples circling this beautiful, round orb embedded with microscopic dust, hand oils, and dirt particles from years upon years of protracted use that, in many cases, verged on abuse. But somehow, amid the dirt and hand grease, this leather has held up.

The tips of my fingers on my right hand rest softly against the leather, gently, with fingers raised so the ball does not sit entirely in my palm. My left hand, the right hand's attendant guide on the journey into flight, sits vertically, providing a human ballast for the ball as it sits in comfortable unison with my right hand, over my shoulder, horizontal to my right ear.

I am loaded.

My eyes lock on the front of the rim with the focus and precision of a sniper four miles from his target. No matter what position, predicament, or situation I'm in, I never lose that singular focus on that orange painted piece of steel protruding eighteen inches off that glass backboard.

I am now locked.

My right foot is forward, my left just inches behind, my knees are shoulder-width apart, and my shoulders are square to the rim.

My knees sink, my butt drops like there is a string inside of it pulling my entire body toward the floor. Then, at the exact moment of just enough, my knees, hammies, and glutes slam on the brakes of their descent, instantly reverse direction, and jettison upward. Ironically, my hands do the same in perfect unison. I feel my hand starting to go past my head in perfect sync with my rising knees.

I feel my feet roll forward from my heels to the tips of my toes as I jump into the air. At the apex of my leap, my arms smoothly rise and fully extend into the air. Then, like an instant chain reaction, at the last second, my right hand pushes a millisecond further in front of my guiding left, my right wrist snaps forward, the tips of my fingers flick, my middle finger the last to leave the ball as I release this majestic piece of brown leather into the sky.

And my eyes have never left the front of the rim, but the ball has taken flight.

I take my eyes off the front of the rim for the first time and see this beautiful projectile I have released to the rafters. Its black lines spinning in perfect rotation toward the rim.

My feet land back to the wood floor cushioned by the tight-knit cotton of my NBA emblazoned socks and plastic soles of my Nike high tops, before the ball does. My eyes are now locked on the descending Spalding falling farther and farther toward the rim like a target in the crosshairs of a military video you know will hit its target, until ...

SPLASH! Nylon, baby!

2

THE SMELL OF HOME

It might have started out like many households in America, I suspect. Dad looks at Mom and they agree to get their child in some kind of organized sport. Whether the child has shown some interest or proclivity for it or maybe they are just starting school for the first time, most parents want their child to be part of something, to get exercise, or get to know more people in the community.

Sure, we wanted all those things as we came out of our nesting cocoon of childbirth as so often happens when you have your first few children.

I was already coaching my older son and his friends in his recreation basketball league, called "Swisherball" in our local area, named after its eponymous leader who is the perfect, humble mix of Willy Wonka, a Bible thumpin' preacher, and Diplo. He also happens to be the athletic director of our small private school and also our school's gym teacher so, for our family, he is the epicenter of all recreation, school, and summer basketball camp activities in our lives.

Angie and I have three boys. I coached my oldest son and his friends for six wonderful years. They were all great kids, and we had a blast winning and losing together.

But my middle son, Brock, and his friends are ... different.

As Brock's preschool year was winding down, the school called us into the office. They wanted to meet with us about Brock's progression. We had heard about these meetings. They were generally to inform the parents that their child was not ready for kindergarten. We had heard, through the grapevine, that some parents got wildly offended at these meetings and disagreed with the school's assessment of their child.

We had not been to one of these meetings with our oldest son, so this caused us some mild concern.

Our preschool was led by a sixty-something Oklahoman drill sergeant named Blanche Colquitt. Except this drill sergeant had an engaging personality, a heart of gold, rocked a tight blond bob, and knew her stuff like I know a bag of donut holes.

As a grown-ass man, even I was afraid of her yet respected her to the nth degree. She was legendary in these parts for knowing what a child needed. Kind of a Sacramento celebrity, like royalty really.

Brock was among the youngest in his class with his August 1 birthday. I, being the natural academic, wanted to hold him back so he could be better at sports, as is being repeated all over preschools (and beyond) in and around America to this very day. In many instances this is a smart and necessary choice as boys develop slower than girls, or so I am told.

And I was no different. I wanted to give my son an athletic leg up.

My wife and I went into the conference with Blanche, the kindergarten teacher, and the headmaster of our school. It was a slow march past the administration offices that felt like my wife and I were entering a firing squad, except with really smart, attractive women armed with pencils, pads, and the finest Talbots dresses.

They started by welcoming us with the painted-on smiles of someone about to give you a cancer diagnosis. They analyzed our son's test scores, behavior, and interactions with others in his preschool class. It was formal.

I am looking at my wife thinking *WTF*?

One by one, they kept going through assignments, assessments, and test scores, actually pushing Brock's graded papers in front of our eyes to prove their points. They had clearly done their due diligence on our son, and these were the substantive materials of their oral arguments.

I guess many of the parents are lawyers.

Finally, I could take no more and just jumped in and said, "Hey, look, we are cool with you keeping Brock back. He is young for his class, and there are a lot of older boys in it. We trust you guys, nothing to worry about here."

Their six eyes just looked at me as if waiting for the punch line.

A long awkward beat.

As I mentioned, we had heard the nightmare stories from around our school of parents who took it as a personal affront when it was suggested to them that Junior wasn't ready for kindergarten. For me, I just figured Mrs. Colquitt had seen a shit-ton more children in her professional life than I ever will, so why wouldn't I trust her?

The fiery Sooner looked me right in the eye and with her mellifluous, charming twang said, "No way! No! Oh, no way, Cree-s. You would be doing that child a disservice if you held him back. He is ready. No, he is ready, Cree-s."

Okay, then.

My wife and I looked at each other and nodded. We're good here. Peace out!

And so began our foray into Brock's kindergarten class.

At that moment, I had no idea how much this class of children would impact my life. Sure, I knew I wanted to help coach, to be a part of my son's life, but I had no grander vision. I was already coaching my older son's team and just figured I would play my part, with another dad or two, on my second son's team, and, of course, do the exact same for my third son's team when he was old enough just to keep everything even as parents with multiple children often do.

Man, was I wrong.

This began a nine-year journey with my son and the boys of St. Matthews Day School. A journey that would change my life forever.

JUST BREATHE

The gym looks like many gyms do across America. Six baskets. One at either end of a full-length hoop court and four more if you cut the full court in two. There are tons of kids running around. But we aren't running full court today. We are running half that distance. Two games side-by-side. This is kindergarten basketball in America.

The hoops are lowered to eight feet and then affixed with an apparatus that attaches to the regular basket. It lowers the hoop to six feet so these little guys and girls can more easily make baskets.

It smells, well, it smells like a gym. Musty, dusty, and perhaps the faint hint of Pine-Sol from the previous night's cleaning, if you're lucky.

You don't come here for the smells.

The stands are filled with grandparents, aunts and uncles, moms and dads set to watch the hilarity that is these games: kids running with the ball tucked under their arms, others running the wrong way and shooting at their own baskets, a few others actually doing things correctly.

In our league, each child wears a primary colored sweatband on their wrist: green, yellow, blue, red, and black. The opposing team is given the same wristbands. It is our league's valiant attempt to make certain each child knows who to cover in this man-to-man only league. If you are wearing the red wristband, you cover the child with the same colored wristband who is on the opposing team.

I will admit it, I was a skeptic when I first saw this. Without these sweatband identifiers, it is mayhem on this court of five-year-olds. With these sweatband identifiers, fractionally below mayhem. Some kids get it; others not so much.

Our team gets it. Always has.

A core group who are ready. They have been told what to expect in the few practices we have had prior to this game, and they are now as prepared as a prelaunch Cape Canaveral rocket.

And we fire that rocket onto the court. It is disorganized for sure, but more organized than any other team. These boys have been taught about a brotherhood from day one. "Rely on the brother next to you on the court: play defense, pass selflessly, and make your lay-ups." The basics. The way the game was intended to be played by Dr. Naismith, when he invented basketball in Springfield, Massachusetts (ironically a city, and highway sign, I passed and read every weekend on our way to ski in Vermont).

No, there was no indiscriminate gunning here. No one-on-five here. No glory boys who want to score twenty a game. They have been taught that at this early age. We are stronger together, as one, our five versus their five, any day, any court. All five players, in two separate units, but working together. No standing out on the wing calling for the ball. No! Never. Pick, move, cut, and keep running!

And we roll. And we roll the next game too. And the next game.

These boys are special.

As I stand on the sidelines of this particular game, I stop for a moment and just look around. It's as if the sounds from this packed gym of insanity have gone mute on my own inner monologue. I survey the families in the stands laughing and pointing, some shouting at the top of their lungs, some sitting steadfastly, fuming their child is not more involved in the game; others just grinning. The expressions and thought processes are many and varied.

Then I study the boys and girls running up and down the court. Some as serious as driving to the hoop to win a last-second NBA championship, others jumping up and down with their hands raised calling for the ball, one in the corner picking his nose, and another studying an ant on the outer reaches of the court.

A grin slowly rises across my face like the morning sun in Kailua.

I take a deep breath and breathe the air deep into my lungs. I smell it all: the dust, the sweat, the cleaner, the sweetness of the spilled Gatorade from last week's game that has now solidified under my toes only to have formed a sticky, reddish, glue-like gunk on the soles of my Sauconys.

Again, I breathe the air in deeply to my lungs.

I am in love.

This is my home.

This is where I belong.

3

UNDERPANTS AND
ALLIGATORS

I grew up in a modest 2,200-square-foot house in the 'burbs of New York. My room was small. I shared it with my brother. He was two years older than me.

We had two single beds hugging each wall with a separation in the middle. We shared a nightstand of some cheap lacquered wood and a craned-neck light atop it that would shut us off to our childhood dreams. The room had blue and black carpet covering the entire floor, not the expensive kind with the padding that some people would pay extra for. No, in my room, you could feel the half-inch plywood below your feet when you walked, let alone jumped.

My brother Cary and I called the blue-black distance between our beds the ocean. We would jump from bed to bed pretending there were sea monsters, alligators, and sharks trying to get us. *Jaws* had hit the theaters in the summer of 1975, my tenth year on earth, his twelfth.

To say we had an idyllic childhood seems like bragging. I am bragging. My brother and I created so many different fantasy worlds with our minds in those days of the early to mid-seventies. There were no video games, no iPad, no cell phones.

Our beds not only functioned as "safe harbor" vessels over this carpet ocean, but also as various sorts of imaginary crafts: a spaceship scanning the universe for extraterrestrials to engage in battle, a Sherman tank attacking warring battalions on the battlefield, or a Formula One race car making quick turns around the streets of Monte Carlo. The scenes and scenarios were endless.

We would stack pillows and blankets high atop the bed and snuggle betwixt and between them, always interlocking legs for the security and comfort of a brother (errr, battalion leader), as we imaginary played. It was really a combination of *Rat Patrol*, *Star Wars*, and *Kelly's Heroes* that provided the impetus:

"They're coming up the right flank."

"Ready?"

"Gunner ready, sir."

"Aim!"

"Panzers in sight, sir." (An irony perhaps with our German heritage.)

"Fire!"

To which both of us spewed machine gun sounds from our lips slapping together with our saliva creating the cacophony.

My brother was my best friend.

When you are young, you don't call your brother your friend because your immature mind never thinks you are friends because you are brothers. But my brother was my best friend. Still is. How we played for endless hours in that room, on those beds, using only our imagination and the back and forth dialogue we could come up with. Oh, to be back in those days again. To be back there just one more time with him.

Heaven.

But Cary did not share my enthusiasm for athletics, especially not basketball. In fact, he thought the game was stupid. "What's the point?" His words did not deter me.

When you walked into our room, we had a dresser to the immediate right and a full desk straight ahead. To describe it now makes it seem small and cramped, like really cramped. But as a child, I knew no difference. To me, I was pimpin' la vida loca in that tiny room. (Kids need a lot less than we parents think.)

One Christmas morning when I was ten, I received a Nerf basketball hoop set. But this was not your ordinary Nerf basketball hoop set, ya know, like the one everyone has in which the Nerf balls fit in the palm of your hand. No, this was different.

This Nerf ball was five times the size of the regular little Nerf ball most kids had. This was special. My parents had paid extra for this one. And while not the size of an actual basketball, it was, nonetheless, just a wee bit smaller than a 28.5-inch basketball, so it felt like you were shooting something of substance. This was a rogue Nerf ball.

The set came with the standard cardboard backboard that all Nerf sets come with in which you slide the plastic clamp through the cardboard backboard that enabled you to affix it to the top of most all eight-foot wood house doors.

As God as my witness, I thought that was one of the greatest Christmas gifts I had ever received up to that point in my life.

That Nerf ball let me do things I couldn't do with a regular ball. I could palm it, dunk, and play above the rim, mimicking the guys I saw on TV: Earl "The Pearl" Monroe, Clyde Frazier, and Willis Reed. I played on that thing for hours and invented any number of shots from any number of different positions in my room: off the wall, lying in bed, sitting at my desk, from the floor, you name it.

And when a friend came over, forget it. It was bedlam as we attempted to dunk over each other trying to avoid cracking our heads open on the dresser next to the door that housed my Garanimals and Hanes white Ts. That my mother didn't shut it down more often truly says something about the type of mother she was. She had three boys and she let them dawgs play.

I knew every angle of that room; I had to. We were now at an age where you could block shots on a rim that hung low on that eight-foot door. And by now we were also learning how to power to the rim. You knew you were gonna get creamed by the guy protecting the rim, but it didn't matter. After multiple collisions, bloodshed, and many bags of ice, we were forced to make a rule that you could only block with your head.

The video playback in my mind of those days provides me with smile after smile all these years later.

For my life, this is where it all started. My childhood room, a Christmas gift, and shooting at a cardboard backboard with a foam ball.

THE IDOLS

By now, I, like most kids of my era, had fallen in love with Dr. J., Julius Erving. He was my era's Michael Jordan or LeBron. He was so much more than a basketball player. He was a cultural icon who personified style. He had this massive afro, wore the coolest threads and gear, and he could jump out of the gym. (YouTube that stuff; it's legendary.)

To watch him in those days was something special, especially in his red, white, and blue jerseys with stars on them playing for the New Jersey Nets of the ABA and winning titles in 1974 and our country's bicentennial of 1976. When I was a ten-year-old boy, he was the man. And on my Nerf court in my small room in suburbia, I was him.

While I loved Dr. J., I saw clearly that he was not like me in many ways. So I decided to model my game after a guy who was more like me, who had my body type: a little thicker, a big booty, and someone who never got tired. Adrian Dantley, or "AD," was that guy. He played for University of Notre Dame from 1973 to 1976, and I must have seen him on TV playing for one of the early schools who dominated our television back then.

AD was not that big by basketball standards, maybe 6 foot 5, but he had the sweetest shot and so many low post moves, he could lose anyone. As a youngster, I never had his shot, so I figured I should study his pump fakes and post moves. That, I could do. I thought he was the coolest guy in college, and he went on to have an illustrious NBA career with the Utah Jazz and Detroit Pistons among others. Don't know why it was him, all I can think is that he looked like me. I just loved AD.

As I got a few years older, I started to take notice of our town's high school team because that was a big Friday night out for me. To be in the stands rooting for your high school team was a huge deal in our small town. The gym was electric, and when you brought in a local rival like Byram Hills, forget it. The place was wild, the games always close, and the crowds as maniacal as you can imagine for a gym with a sold-out capacity of 526.

As a young boy, I dreamed of one day playing there. This was our Madison Square Garden, this was our basketball mecca. Oh, to dream one day.

As I started to understand the high school landscape, I invariably ventured out a little wider and saw who was making headlines in the local papers. At this time, where I grew up in Westchester County, New York, we had a perennial powerhouse called Mount Vernon High School (now most famous for being the city where Denzel Washington grew up).

During my youth, they had two brothers named Scooter and Rodney McCray. They were basketball in Westchester. Older by one year, Scooter became the New York State Player of the Year in his senior year and got recruited by Denny Crum to play at Louisville. That was big-time for Westchester County.

A year later his brother, Rodney, joined him at Louisville, and they went on to win the college basketball championship in 1980. Knowing the McCray brothers came from Westchester somehow made it seem plausible that a kid from our area could play major college basketball even if Pleasantville (oh, yeah, I said Pleasantville) wasn't exactly Mount Vernon.

The crazier thing with the McCray brothers was that they had joined a team with my new favorite college basketball player (now that AD was in the NBA). A guy who had an insane vert named Darrell Griffith. Due to his unreal leaping ability, and insane dunks, he earned the nickname Dr. Dunkenstein.

Since ESPN had just started in September 1979, my early years of *SportsCenter* highlights were replete with Dr. Dunkenstein's exploits. And for me, as a sports nut, I thought whoever created this channel must be a genius, like smarter than Einstein and Madame Curie combined. A show filled with just sports highlights? I mean, I had always been a fan of *Football Follies* and *The George Michael Sports Machine* that aired on Friday and Sunday nights, respectively, but this, this was madness. Who were these *SportsCenter* sport savants?

Wherever we are, whatever sport is ours, we become that idol in our mind's make-believe journey. We are him (or her) for a moment, for that moment in time, in our bedrooms, on the blacktop, in gyms across the globe. This is how it all starts for most of us, the love.

You see someone on TV and mimic that moment in time: a thunderous dunk that shatters a backboard, a last-second shot hanging forever in the air with a defender in your face, a penalty kick to win it, taking off your shirt and sliding to your knees in celebration, a clutch home run while limping around the base paths, a touchdown catch on the tips of your fingers in the back of the end zone to destroy a rival's dreams. The love of something that you enjoy for whatever moment in time.

For me and basketball, that love has never ended ... just changed.

4

CORN DOGS AND FRIES
ARE A GOOD WAY TO DIE

My son Brock attends an independent school of 248 students in Northern California, pre-K through eighth grade. We are mostly middle class and higher with a semi-diverse mix of doctors, dentists, lawyers, lobbyists, real estate professionals, entrepreneurs, and a few peripheral celebrities like Sacramento Kings coach Luke Walton's kids.

There are a total of twelve boys in my son's eighth-grade class. It's 2019, and our team consists of nine of those boys and one seventh grader, a child who will become the best basketball player of all of us. We are seven Caucasians and two African Americans, not that it matters or has ever mattered.

We are a tiny school by any standards, but maybe somehow we are a microcosm of what is happening all over the world with teams playing basketball, or any sport for that matter. These are a group of boys putting their individual needs and desires behind for one more year to work together toward a common unified goal for their school.

That means something to us, to all of us.

OUR HISTORY

Are you kidding me? Who keeps track of these things?

We are 61–6 in our league's history:
First grade 6–0
Second grade 6–0
Third grade 8–0
Fourth grade 8–0
Fifth grade 16–5
Sixth grade 17–1 (three tournament championships)

I know, the absurdity of knowing these things. That man needs a life. Go fishing, for god sakes!

But see, that's just it. My children are my life. I know it's not healthy. But this is my fried food that, although I know it will lead to my demise, I cannot stop consuming—being with my children and their friends.

Yes, I know it will kill me; not literally, of course, but I know it will kill me psychologically. I see it as clear as day. I tell people about it all the time. I am that prescient. I can literally see my downfall in front of me, yet like the car crash you cannot turn away from, I will never turn away from this impending crash of being with my kids until my last child graduates and goes off to start a life for himself.

I know it's coming, but I want to enjoy what we have now. What we have shared together with each of my sons. I don't care what happens to me later because of it. I am here now, in this moment. In this moment with them.

And why? Why do I feel so strongly about this? Because I have seen the other side.

I have spent over sixteen years owning a funeral home, and I have seen what happens to us all. I have distinctly heard the surviving families' prophetic and enduring advice: "Enjoy. They are only young once."

I know I am not alone in hearing this. I am not special in any way. The only aspect that is different about me is that I am heeding those exact words, their advice. I have taken their words not only to heart, but to practice.

I know. I know it will kill me when my kids are gone. My wife even laughs about it. But I am prepared for that kind of death—the one with a smile on.

Don't cry for me, Sacramento!

Now to be fair and honest, our team has been to many AAU tournaments, for the first few years, always together. We won some tournaments and we lost many. It always made us better. Markedly better. What was unique about our team is that we were mostly all kids from the same small school.

Generally, the other teams we were playing were arranged as all-star teams from a certain geographic area, super teams really. We were just eight kids from the same school and a few friends we met along the way. That's what made us better. The fact that we knew each other in other settings, played at each other's houses, went to school together, had sleepovers—these boys got to know each other's personalities.

That was our secret sauce for a small moment in time.

THE CREW

With children it is often difficult to know when they were up past their normal bedtime playing Fortnite, NBA 2K, or Madden. If they got up too early. If one was fighting with his parents or classmates. Was doing poorly in school. If he was worried about starting. So many things can affect a child.

The strange thing is after a few years with them, I know these boys. I can see when they are tired. I can see by their eyes. It shows on their faces, their body language, their giddyup on the court in practice.

They are my family at this point, my surrogate sons. I want you to meet them.

Tim has always been the most aggressive kid on our team. Always. It is in his DNA, not learned. He is a fighter. Nothing dirty, just competitive as hell, and he fears no one no matter the size, color of their skin, or where they come from. He simply has no fear. He is, coincidentally, not the best basketball player skill-wise, but his aggressiveness and tenacity have always made him one of the top players in any league in which he played. When the game is over, he is a different human being: kind, respectful, cheerful, happy. On the court, a cheetah on the Serengeti tracking an unsuspecting baby antelope stuck in the mud at a watering hole.

His parents are among our best friends. Quincy and I have coached together for the last few years, and they have been in our lives since our older children were in kindergarten—now over eleven years of friendship. Tim's dad and mom went through a divorce a few years back, and it was awful. The first of your friends who you would never suspect until you witness it along with them—from afar. They are both good people, caring, loving, and great parents who place their children first, but they weren't good together. We love them both and hang out with them both.

Allison, or "A-Love" as she is to a select few, ironically grew up with pro basketball player Dwayne Wade's current wife, actress Gabrielle Union. Allison is an insanely hardworking woman and a great, not good, great mother. I respect her to the moon and back. Quincy is a great observer of our team. He tells me when I am being too harsh and when we need to push the boys. He has the gift of knowing. There is simply no way I can see all the nuances of each boy, every night. I am grateful for his friendship and how much time he gives to be with his son.

Stevie is the natural. A phenomenal athlete and really good at basketball and football in particular. He is a handsome child and has a cheery personality, always a big smile on his face. His mother was a beauty queen and his father is equally as handsome and a former D-1 wide receiver. Early in our careers, his father, Roger, and I co-coached basketball together. I now assist him in flag football, and he assists Quincy and me in hoops.

We have been together since preschool and have a nice coaching relationship. Both of us have strong, competitive personalities—the type of on-court/field personalities that opposing parents generally detest. I can clearly see that, and I get it. Our problem is that we are all in. We are not interested in holding Johnny's hand through athletics but would rather teach the child the fundamentals and strategy of a sport and, perhaps, the harder life lessons that sometimes accompany it. Roger was raised by a military father and I by a German. Enough said. We try not to be too harsh.

This balance is the trickiest in sports and gets progressively more difficult as the children age.

Roger and his wife, Mariyam, have recently gone through a divorce. Again, horrible for everyone involved. My heart hurts for the kids. Stevie has always been among the top two players in any league he played in, especially as a younger child. Now, in his eighth-grade year, the league talent has caught up to him. He is still a great player, but his confidence has waned over the years, due in no small part, I suspect, to the divorce.

With Stevie, in particular, I see a child I want to protect. I want to help him through this tumultuous road of life because I know it can be tough. While his smile will light up a room, I just know there is something far more vulnerable underneath.

His older sister Kimba is a D-2 college basketball prospect and leads one of the most competitive women's basketball teams in the greater Sacramento area, St. Benedict Preparatory School. She is an excellent student and will, most likely, receive academic as well as athletic scholarships. She is as kind and bubbly as she is a good athlete. Thankfully for Stevie she is a woman, so it is less difficult to live up to. We all look up to Kimba as I know her younger brother does.

Alex is my big man. He came to us in fifth grade and made us markedly better. He is a baseball stud. You watch. A pitcher with a pitcher's calm demeanor, and he can rake to boot. His fastball is legendary, especially when he puts the first one behind your ear. I have seen many boys with shivering knees when they stepped into the batter's box against him.

He is a supreme overall athlete and transitions to basketball with effortless ease. What he lacks, and to some extent, has always lacked, is the killer mentality most coaches want in a big man. He glides down the court, is all finesse around the rim, and doesn't like to bang like a quintessential big man. That was until he hit fourteen. Now, his body is changing as is his mentality on the court. He is becoming more aggressive and it is noticeable. He will be either the best player in our league or among the best by the time it is all said and done.

But Alex has also always had an innate kindness. He has gone out of his way to include my younger son and always make him feel welcome. (My younger son—four years their junior—comes to almost all of our practices and feels like a million bucks hanging out with these older boys on his big brother's team.)

Alex knows this is my favorite part about him. How many older boys can put aside their own sense of machismo and insecurity for a moment and make a younger child feel special by just giving them a high five and a few words of encouragement? The mark of a great human being, and we are raising human beings here.

Alex's dad is a former rocker / diving instructor / artist who works the docks in Oakland. I find him one of the more interesting guys around: no bullshit, no airs, just Howard. A great dude. His wife is a homemaker and a god-fearing woman who loves her son. Her father played professional baseball, so she knows all about that life and what it entails. It wasn't always pretty. She is a great mother: kind, compassionate, positive, and religious, and you can see her instilling these most vital qualities in her son. Howard spends more than half the week in the Bay Area working but tries like hell to get to every game. They are a great American family whom I admire. They will be friends for life.

Dylan came to us in third grade. He is a tall, skinny kid who mans the front of our press. He has twin older siblings, a brother and sister, five years his senior; he is the caboose of the family. As such, he has grown up perhaps more quickly than most of the boys and has the smartass personality to prove it. He has also improved the most over the years due to his parents' desire, his work ethic, and older siblings who have shown him the way. When he gets going, he has one of the deadliest shots in our league when only two years prior it was almost nonexistent.

His parents—ahhh, his parents—some of the supreme benefactors of our school. They worked at a computer company almost thirty years ago and saw something the former owner didn't or didn't want to. So they bought the company and turned it into a multimillion-dollar juggernaut. They are overly generous with giving and making certain the team (and our school) has everything we need. They are quick to pick up food and bar bills and generally want only the best for all of us and their son.

And this influence comes with access. To the school, decision-making, coaching—you get the idea. It is not bad, it is simply the reality, and they will do anything they can to further their children's athletic abilities, and have. I love them. I truly love them not only for how much they do for our school but, more importantly, for the fact that, despite their means and influence, all of their children are kind, respectful, and engaging. To me, this is family, and they are doing something very right.

My son **Brock** is the runt of the litter. The youngest on the team and the most tentative over the years. He has benefited, more than anyone, by playing and being friends with these boys. He has seen their aggressiveness and tried to match it, not because it is anything innately within his persona, but more because he knows he needs to get with the program if he wants to play. And that's just it. He must perform.

I am not that father who has started his son because he is my son. He has earned it. All of my sons know that. We talk about it all the time. My oldest son, Hudson, rode the pines, so has Brock, so will Mack if they aren't among the best five. I just can't be that guy, because I hated that guy growing up. I saw it. I saw it all too often. And kids see it too. They know. You might think they don't, but they are way smarter than parents give them credit for. They see everything.

In fact, one of the greatest coaching compliments I have ever received to this day was from one of Hud's friends, Cole. He said he likes Coach Meyer because he screams at his son just as much as he screams at the rest of us. Cole knows that made me feel good to hear those words. And Cole could fill it! (He made me write that.)

Brock has worked extremely hard on his game, and the result is that he has grown significantly better. Recently, he was not chosen for the better of the three AAU teams in our area and our other starting four were. He didn't like that. I remember him being on the verge of tears when it happened.

Sure, I could've called the local AAU coaches and asked if they could move my son up so he could play with his friends. I had that influence, that street cred, by now locally.

But that's not me.

I wanted to see what my son was made of. It was a pivotal point for me in his growth. Would he just recess into his video game world or would he fight?

He fought.

And Brock and I worked. We worked together. I remember taking a twelve-foot ladder out of our garage and placing it at the top of the key. He looked at me like what the hell are you doing? I wanted to simulate a defender in his face as he shot. I made him pretend he was coming off the pick (the ladder) and try to shoot a three. He thought I was insane, but he did it.

And Brock grinded.

And he got better. He and our sixth man, Nick, developed a nice friendship on their AAU team, and I believe they both benefited in a way they never would have if they had played on the better team. He wants it. He sees his shot falling, he watches the precision of his jay, the rotation of the lines of the ball spinning perfectly in the air. The perfect form. It has been a joy to witness his transformation.

I am proud of how hard he has worked.

Nicholas (Nick) is a lumbering man-child of a boy with a soft left. He has been with us since kindergarten too. His parents are also divorced, and his dad is one of the foremost residential real estate minds and lenders in the United States. To us he is just Stanley. Despite his busy schedule, Stanley has always been gracious to me. He, more than anyone, has always sidled up to me at a party, looked me right in the eye, and said how much he appreciates all I do for these boys. He knows. And I really appreciate that acknowledgment, that articulation to my face. He tells people from his work, from our school, really anyone who will listen about the time I spend with these boys. I am grateful for that because all I have ever wanted was to be involved in my sons' and their friends' lives.

Coaching just gave me more time to do that. The added gift of getting to know my sons' friends and their parents and watch them truly get better year after year is as unique an experience as a human can witness. Think of that: being involved in a group of children's lives from kindergarten through eighth grade, as they grow up, as you see them mature, their idiosyncrasies, their tendencies, their budding personalities, how utterly beautiful, how utterly fantastic! How many parents can say that in their lifetimes?

What an amazing gift I have been given. I am so thankful.

When we started, Nick had a hard time dribbling and running at the same time. His mother, a former D-1 volleyball star, has instilled, if not demanded, he improve his skill set. He tried football but soon gravitated to basketball. He has been to the finest coaches and played on the best AAU teams in our area. He has even been given personal one-on-one tips by former Sacramento Kings great, Bobby Jackson, through his mother's friendship with Bobby. She is a hoop mom tour de force, stopping at nothing to make her son better. And she has.

He has made tremendous growth in his years and will become a dominant force on our team due to his massive size and soft touch around the rim. Seeing his growth, and playing a small part in it, is more gratifying to me than any business deal I could ever close. I am impacting my son's life and his friends' lives. I know I am.

Periodically, I think back to all the men who sacrificed their time and taught me sports growing up. I know how I feel about all of those men. To be thought of like that would be a legacy I want to leave with my children and their friends in my short time on this earth. I know these boys don't know that right now. I know they don't know how special this time is. How can a fourteen-year-old articulate those feelings?

But I know they will in retrospect. When they are older, wiser, more in tune with their feelings and emotions as grown men. I know they will feel, like me, that coaches play such an absolutely instrumental and vital role in boys' (and girls') lives growing up, like Coach Tony Dovi in my own childhood.

I know they will.

James is not a basketball player. He is built differently than most kids of this age. He has that innate hyper-aggressiveness you want in an athlete. He is a phenom in soccer, lacrosse, and football, all sports that more clearly align with his talents. There is no basketball in this boy's future. I know that and James knows that. We've talked about it, even joked about it. Yet I know he will be pivotal to our team.

He is an alpha male on a team of finesse players. And we need an alpha. Even if it is only for a few minutes a game to set the tone, dive on the floor, play in-your-face defense, I don't care. I need him on our team for his tenacity. The others see it and they become more tenacious. That's how you build a team.

Lastly, there is **Ben**. Ben has been on and off our team since kindergarten. He is simply a great kid, everybody's friend, funny, kind, warm, and genuine. His basketball skills are not quite where the others are, but he plays solid D and can pass with the best of them. Everyone loves Ben for his chill personality and easy-going attitude.

His dad is a musician for a famous rock band from the '90s. His mom is a yogi. They too were divorced during our tenure together. As all children are, Ben and his brothers were affected. They are great boys. We need Ben on our team because he is our glue. We stick together because of Ben.

Brock, Stevie, Tim, Nicholas, Ben, and James have been with me since kindergarten. Dylan came in third grade. Alex in fifth. It is a long time with a core group working together as one.

THE TOURNIQUET

In the early years, the key to their success was the way they pressed. We had two basic presses. A 1 x 2 x 2 called Crush It and a 3 x 2 we called LAX. I taught these to the boys early in their career. I am only slightly ashamed to say we started playing AAU in third grade.

I said only slightly ashamed.

The boys took to it like fish to water. For whatever reason, they just got it. And it all started from a simple but profound rationale that I heard watching Sacramento Kings owner Vivek Ranadivé describe on a YouTube video when discussing coaching his daughter's team. It went something like this:

After we score a bucket and the other team has to throw in the ball, how many of the opposing team are on the court?

Correct answer: 4 (as one of the opposing team's players must throw the ball in from out of bounds).

Next question, how many of our players are on the court?

Correct answer: 5

Now, if we are playing five of us versus four of them every time we score a basket, we should win in that scenario almost every time, right?

Correct answer: Yes.

And we did ... repeatedly.

In our earlier years, we created so much hysteria, imbalance, and controlled chaos each and every time we scored, it would not be unusual to go up ten to fourteen points in less than two minutes. It was that much of a game changer.

And that was because of four things: everyone had very specific roles, they knew how to execute their roles via repetition, they were unselfish, and they got every loose ball.

Each position of the press must have the player with the right kind of personality for that position. It is not simply put the best five on the court and see them thrive. No, to understand the press properly is to place the personality best suited for each individual position on the court. I take into account personalities, siblings, parents, desire, and, lastly, skill. It is less about skill and more about knowing what to do with it in a press. Sounds ridiculous, but it's true.

Let me explain—

In our 3 x 2 base press, my son played the left front on the inbounding side of the ball. His job was simple. Never let anyone come up the baseline to your left. NEVER! That gets broken down and the whole press gets shitcanned. He knew how to use the colored strip to the left of him as another defender to make the dribbler step out of bounds for a turnover or, in most cases, to help drive the dibbler back to the center of the court where his other brother would be waiting.

His personality fit the left front perfectly. A smart, calculating pragmatist in everything he does, Brock knows how to follow the letter and spirit of instruction, whether it be homework, directions in school, or the front left corner of the press. He was steadfast and brilliant at his job.

Dylan, the octopus, our lanky smartass, played the middle of the press as deftly as a Rodeo Drive plastic surgeon did rhinoplasty. He trusted implicitly that Brock would refuse to give up that baseline (he heard Brock's dad scream it too many times at practice). So what would invariably happen at this level of basketball is the dribbler would have his head down and then see Brock cutting him off at the sideline, he would slow down, and reverse direction to the middle of the court.

Dylan had seen this movie a hundred times before, way before the dribbler came to that realization in his own mind, so he had already been drifting to that side of the court as the dribbler was trying to beat Brock up the side, knowing Brock was about to make him reverse direction, and he (Dylan) needed to be there waiting for the kill.

And he would always be there waiting for the trap that he and Brock would then clamp down on the dribbler.

At the same time, the right corner of the press would be occupied by Tim, the most aggressive of the group. Tim, the hyena, would be on the right front of the 3 x 2 press, the farthest away from the inbounding ball, and he would gravitate more to the middle. No inbounder would try to throw that long pass in front of Tim because they knew how fast he was, and he would simply jump the pass, pick it off, take two steps, and lay it in for an easy bucket.

Teams learned not to throw that pass after an attempt or two, so Tim would hang more to the middle waiting to see what Dylan did and then pounce on the second or third potential free man for the steal. He, and his aggressiveness, were in many ways the keys to the press. Tim knew he was the weak side of the press, but there was nothing weak about his side.

As he'd watch Brock cut off the baseline and Dylan slowly creep to Brock's side of the court, Tim would similarly slide to the middle where another opponent would be patiently waiting in an attempt to receive the ball from his now trapped dribbler. Tim would sit behind him and wait for the dribbler to throw the ball to his teammate in the middle. Then Tim would step in front, pick off the ball and make an easy lay-up or, if blocked at the rim miraculously by the inbounder, reset the offense for our next play.

Generally these were all lay-ups by us because everyone knew that ball was not getting over half court, so their tendency was to get ready to pounce on the next pass and attack the rim for a lay-up, rebound, or put back.

The way the press unfolded was artistry really.

The second row of the press was equally as impressive. Stevie played behind Brock on the side of the inbounding ball, roughly at the three-point line. His job was that of a free safety on the football field, a position Stevie played (along with quarterbacking) since first grade on the gridiron. A free safety in football watches the quarterback's eyes and breaks on the ball.

On the basketball court, Stevie was supposed to sit back and watch the initial dribbler and try to cut off any secondary or tertiary options to whom that dribbler might be seeking to pass. He knew the dribbler wasn't getting by Brock. He knew Dylan's long arms were going to close on him, he knew Tim was getting the next short pass. He knew the middle of the court or a soft attempted lob over Brock and Dylan would be the next likely option.

He would cut off the second or third pass and then drive to the hoop, get fouled or dish to Dylan, Tim, or Brock for an uncontested lay-up.

It was madness really.

When we were causing turnover after turnover, opposing coaches would invariably call a time-out to stop our momentum, calm his team down, and then quickly show them how to break the press they were seeing.

When this happened, our boys knew we would then immediately switch presses to give them a totally different look.

The boys had a sixth sense. I don't attribute this to my coaching at all as much as I believe, after a while, they simply could smell blood in the water.

They knew which teams couldn't handle the pressure, they knew which kids would crack, they knew where the other team wanted to go. After all this time, the competition was mostly the same kids they had seen before. They could smell fear.

The final position on the court was the weak side back. Alex held down this position. His main responsibility was to not let anyone get behind him. He was a very athletic big so he could bait people into thinking they could throw it deep, only to pick the ball off and dribble back down the court.

I am fairly certain Alex was troubled back there, wanting to get into the action of the street fight that was happening in front of him.

It was all too often that the ball would never even get to him, and he was seemingly out of the play as our safety valve at the back of the press watching the madness unfold in front of him.

To this day, he never complained about it. He knew we were a team and he was cool with it. I tried to draw things up for him on offense because I knew he needed to be fed too.

You gotta do this as a coach when everyone can play. Everyone needs to eat. Everyone wants to be on *SportsCenter*.

But that's my job.

The one principle I have stressed from day one is selflessness—not caring about scoring on a team of such strong personalities. We never once talked about scoring. We talked about selflessly finding the open man and playing defense. Up until this year, our final year before high school, everyone bought in effortlessly. There were games I would have refs come up to me after a game and say, "I have never seen a bunch of young kids pass so much."

To me, the greatest compliment as a coach.

And it was true. Our boys didn't care. Sure everyone wanted to be on the all-tourney team and get the cheesy T-shirt that came along with such an honor. I got that. But I never cared and attempted to quash any individual or selfish behavior on the court. And they tried. Trust me they tried. We all realize that parents are barking in their son's ear on each and every car ride home or at every dinner table or every drive to and from practice.

We all want our son to be the man.

But you know what? Life isn't like that. Life is about working with each other, whether a teammate, family, a coworker, whomever, to make the team better. And teams are better when the players work together. And that is a difficult concept to teach a child-athlete.

I credit our parents and coaches for helping me reinforce this to our boys. Sure, we screamed it from the top of our lungs at almost every practice. Sure we sat people who didn't pass to a clearly open man, and over the years the boys understood that this teamwork was their greatness, this was what made them so good. This was the key to their success.

How is this even possible when we turn on *SportsCenter* and all we hear about are the dunks and who scored the most? We live in a highlight-reel society when the true greatness of a team is selflessness. It is putting the team above your own needs for the greater good. It is a massive challenge that some handle better than others.

These were ten kids who played their parts to perfection, and they knew their aggressiveness would only feed into the hysteria of the moment. Hysterics create bad decisions. Bad decisions are what we fed on.

5

A THING OF COMPLETE
AND UTTER BEAUTY

I walked down the antiseptic hallway of the heavily waxed laminate floors of my middle school. In my hand was a hall pass to go to the bathroom from my sixth-grade English teacher. As I walked to the bathroom door, I remember hearing in the faint distance: Bam. Bam. Bam.

A basketball hitting the floor.

And as if in some modern day, suburban folk tale, I found myself inexplicably pulled toward these deceptively seductive, mellifluous sounds like a rat to the Pied Piper's magic pipe; only here that tune was a basketball hitting the hardwood.

I stopped at the gym door and slowly peered my head in, knowing, in the back of my mind, I was on my English teacher's internal time clock for bathroom hall passes from his class. Somehow now I didn't care. I, like the rat, was transfixed to that sound. I would have followed it anywhere.

Bam. Bam. Bam.

And what I saw as I peered my head into that gym was the sweetest act I had ever seen in my young life up to that point—a thing of complete and utter beauty.

The perfect jump shot.

It was literally perfect form. The squaring of the shoulders. The legs bending at the knees. The legs rising in perfect unison. The elbow up. That subtle flick at the top. The same release point every. Single. Time. The perfect rotation. And it was all so effortless. Time after time, the exact same motion, the exact same ball release. Complete perfection!

And when the ball descended and snapped the nylon, it made one of the sweetest sounds on this earth.

Not the typical swish, but more like a poof. Poof. Poof.

No rim, no backboard, nothing but fabric. Repeatedly. The sound of the leather ball rotating perfecting through the air and hitting a worn piece of nylon in an old middle school gym smelling of dust and mildew was my first experience of love outside my own family. And that sound was intoxicating. For me, even to this very day, markedly more intoxicating than any spirit that has ever crossed my lips.

And watching shot after shot of that perfect form, the spinning of that leather, the look of that rotation and never hitting anything but nylon netting, that was it. It was fascinating to witness, but as I close my eyes today, I can still fully hear, see, and feel the snapping of that net. Poof, poof, poof.

Seeing this at a young age was really poetry to me. It was Yeats, it was Keats, it was Poe, it was Angelou all in one.

I was hooked.

I honestly don't think I ever saw him miss a foul shot.

The rumor was he played on Long Island. The rumor was he played against Julius Erving, known to every single one of us as the now famous Dr. J. But this was years before the internet, so facts couldn't be substantiated on the spot. I only, much later in life, came to find out that he, my middle school gym teacher, Jim Bergholtz, not only played against, but was the co-high school player of the year on Long Island when he played for Hicksville High and Dr. J was at Roosevelt.

How could that be?

How could Dr. J be my idol, the guy whose posters adorned my childhood bedroom, and the sole reason I bought the Converse sneakers he endorsed and why I attempted to grow an afro as a suburban white child from Pleasantville, New York? How could his co-player of the year in high school be my very own middle school gym teacher?

Are you %$#^* kidding me?

But so it was.

And this is where it all started for me—in person.

The Pleasantville Middle School gym. This is where the imagination and indoor childhood bedroom skills from my Nerf basketball court on that blue and black carpet of ocean on Hillview Drive would now be put to the test in a real-life gym, with regulation-sized hoops and aged, varnished hardwood.

This is where I truly fell in love with the game.

Where my now pot-bellied gym teacher, a former Long Island high school basketball legend would play pickup games with us in his regular street clothes. Which I later thought was his way of saying I am not even gonna break a sweat, punk—a small FU to us youngsters he was playing with at the time.

And to his real credit, he never once went to the rack. NEVER! That would be too unfair as a grown man against his middle school competition. Nope, he just stopped and popped—from deep. Beyond the three-point line before there was a three-point line; this with two, maybe three, kids hangin' on him. To this day, the single most beautiful shot I have ever seen released from a hand right in front of my grill.

This dust-filled hardwood floor with poor ventilation and a band stage too close underneath one of the baskets and a padded brick wall too close to the other wall was my poetry. I knew that. I knew the way it made me feel deep within my soul. I knew the way it made me feel after playing. The joy.

Remembering each of my great plays in my head with a smile. Thinking what I could improve on. How to stop the guy that beat me three times to the baseline. How to stop that stop and pop in my face. Sure, that kid was a few years older, I would think, but I could shut that down.

I wasn't even that good at the game. That's the funny part. Not even near the best player in my own grade. But it didn't matter to me. It's what I loved. It's the relationship I wanted to have. It's what brought me my joy.

And it all started with seeing that thing of complete and utter beauty. Poof.

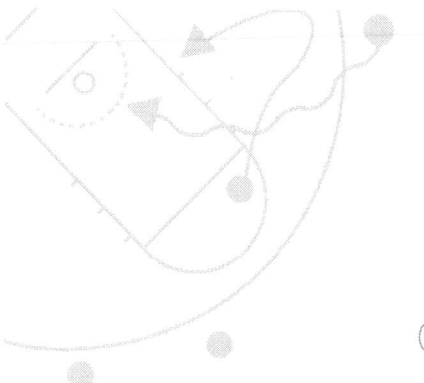

6

A YEAR TO REMEMBER

Their seventh-grade year was challenging. They had been coached by me for the past seven years. They had a lot of success. They were comfortable with me, knew what to expect.

I knew our school had brought in a friend of our AD who had won a league championship at our rival school. He was brought over to teach and take the controls of the varsity competitive team, our school's A-team. The same thing happened with my older son's team. I was forced to give up the reins, so I knew it was coming. I knew my coaching life had a ceiling at our school.

I was okay with that, I thought.

Coaching took a lot of time, and we coaches had to work really hard to be good at it, like anything in life.

As the boys entered their seventh-grade year of flag football in the fall, I knew I should enjoy our last time together. The next season, a few short months away, I would be handing them over to their new coach for the upcoming basketball season. When I was officially told by our athletic director that the transition was definitely happening, I was sad.

Sure, I knew it was coming, but hearing the actual words was difficult. These boys were part of my family, even more than my older son's friends because of our long history together—so many more games on the weekends, the battles, the wars, the hours in the gym. I regularly found myself looking forward to going to practice and seeing them.

As word slowly spread, many of the boys heading into the seventh grade were equally sad that I was not coaching. In many ways, I was really the only basketball coach they ever knew.

"Coach, you not gonna coach us?" Stevie asked looking right into my eyes.

"I ... I ... I think it's Coach Applewhite this year."

But, Coach—," Tim said.

"I ..."

The two boys just stood there and looked at me. My two stars from all these years. I saw the vulnerability on their young faces, the genuine sadness you can see from a child. I saw they want me to coach. My heart hurt. These boys, they know our squad belongs together.

We just sat there staring at each other for an awkward beat.

"Coach, *you're* our coach," Stevie said.

I simply said not this year and forced a laugh. I told them I was going to miss them and encouraged them to get after it. They knew they had to be strong and learn from a new coach. I tried to stay strong and be positive, but my heart hurt and I think the boys could tell. I know they could tell by just the way they looked at me.

When their new coach called a meeting of all the families to discuss the upcoming basketball season, I knew I should keep my distance out of respect, so my wife attended. He started off with, "I am not here to win a championship. I am here to teach the boys basketball and have fun."

And with that simple phrase, he lost the room. They say the first rule of public speaking is to know your audience.

Coach Applewhite was a good coach, a real Xs and Os guy. I need to be clear about this. He is a very good basketball coach. However, his style could not have been more polar opposite to mine: I was run and gun, press everywhere, haphazard and frenzied, play on instinct and tenacity. He was methodical, never pressed, even paced, and ran a set offense until it yielded an opportunity.

I sat at the first few games that year biting the inside of my cheek and slowly tasted my type O negative in my saliva, the result of my overzealous mouth gnawing. When he didn't play the kids I thought were better than anyone on the court, I hurt for those boys. My boys. I literally felt their pain. I knew what they were capable of. I knew how they were reacting inside their young minds. They started to disengage. You could see it on their faces as they slumped at the end of the bench.

The first few loses is when it started. Parents chirping after the games. An idle comment here, another in passing there. Then, asking my opinion of things. And finally, outright calling me on the phone and demanding I lead a charged insurrection to the AD's office with pickaxes and fire torches. The undercurrent was thick, like real thick. Everyone in the gym could feel it.

I am not going to lie, it made me feel wanted again. It's not that I wanted anyone to fail. It's just ... I just ... I wanted those boys to be coached by someone who gave it all he had. Who was all in. Who would go that extra mile, those extra weekend practices, show the passion, the fire I felt these boys deserved to try to win a banner. They deserved a coach who would push them to try to win every game, even when they were the underdog. To try new things, something different, press, zone, different lineups, something, anything.

As league play started, Coach needed parents to be scorekeepers as part of our parochial league duties (parents fill in to save costs). When I saw him walking toward me, I looked at my phone to avoid eye contact. Out of my peripheral view I could see the figure in front of me wasn't moving. I looked up. He asked if I could help. Now I was going to keep stats and, in doing so, be right there on the floor next to the team.

I thought this was a really bad idea. But looking around the gym, I saw no one else. I was not the kinda guy to keep my mouth shut, although I fully knew I should. This was like placing a wolf in the henhouse.

At first, I tried to keep my words to encouragement, but as I watched this methodical, slow-paced offense play out like some Harlem Globetrotter passing exhibition, I often found myself shouting, "Go to the damn rack!" They were clearly running a set offense and passing and passing and passing …

No one ever shot.

When one of the female teachers from our school whose son played point guard turned to me in the middle of the game and said, "Is this normal?" I burst out laughing. Even the neophyte observer could tell something was drastically amiss.

In fact, it bordered on the absurd. And when my point guard Stevie came down the court on a fast break, stopped, and ripped a three as he would have less than ten months prior with me screaming at the top of my massive lungs to "pull the trigger," he was immediately pulled from this game for doing so.

He was yanked from the game for shooting!

There was a new sheriff in town, and their coach was making a statement. And we parents all heard it loud and clear.

My son was unhappy. He wanted to quit. Of course he did. His father had coached him since kindergarten. He loved having me coach. We laughed and joked a lot, talking about our games, practices, and opponents. It was our thing together—father and son.

Our quiet talks around bedtime were always the best. He was tired and loved to share with me the stories of his day. In one of our talks, he told me the older boys at school called me "a legend."

"A legend?" I would say curiously.

And the story goes like this: When Brock was in fourth grade, our AD asked me to coach the eighth-grade team one night because their coach called in sick at the last minute. It was a rainy Friday night in which I would have rather stayed home, but I drove the half hour because the school needed me.

When I walked into the gym, I recognized a few of the eighth-grade boys from previously coaching them in flag football. They smiled and were psyched when I told them I was coaching that evening. I didn't know any of their plays or what their coach expected of them, so I just went in there and winged it.

The game was insane: fast-paced, run and gun, and hard fought. It was close, but, in the end, we came out victorious. I thanked the boys and went on my merry way.

One woman, whose son is now at the IMG Academy in Florida, came up and grabbed my arm: "Coach!"

I turned to her and smiled. She just stood there shaking her head.

"Coach, I have always heard," she said in shock or awe. "I mean, I heard what they all said about your coaching but—"

"A little intense, right?"

She gave me a hug.

"Thank you. Thank you for coming out here and bringing that passion to our boys. Thank you." She pulled back and couldn't stop shaking her head and staring at me.

What I didn't realize until many months later, after the basketball season was long over, was that we had beaten the first-place team that evening and that was our team's only victory that year. In the hallways between classes at our small school, the eighth graders told Brock and Hud, "Your dad is a legend." Heady stuff coming from upperclassmen who rarely even acknowledged underclassmen. My sons beamed hearing those words.

One game and I'm a legend.

So, of course, I knew Brock wasn't going to love his new coach. I understood. But I told Brock it was the best thing for him. He will see what an objective party thinks of his game. And when Coach took him aside and told him he could play on the rec team (our school's B team) or the comp team and maybe not play as much, Brock saw where he stood with this man, with the basketball world really.

And for me, this was one of the crossroads of my son's young life. He wasn't offended at all. He knew he could play on the rec team and be the leading scorer and have fun with his friends or he could be one of the last kids on the bench on the comp team and work to get better, to play with kids mostly better than he was.

His choice at twelve years old.

We talked about it. He weighed everything evenly. (He is his mother's son.) My wife chimed in her opinion. I chimed in mine. He did his own balancing test and decided he wanted to play on the comp team.

For me, this decision showed me a great deal about my son.

Did he want to be the man on a team where he knew he could coast or was he up for the challenge of getting better with no promise of playing time?

He chose the challenge.

Very interesting how small moments in your children's lives tell you a great deal about who they will become.

The season did not end well. The team was 8–10. Well, that's not entirely true. They won the championship … of the silver division. Our league decided all teams deserved a chance to play in a tournament atmosphere; of course it did, in our "everyone gets a trophy" society. So they constructed two separate tournaments. The top sixteen teams in the gold division. The bottom ten in the silver division. Our boys won the silver division in thrilling last-second fashion. We have a school banner and everything. It was an exciting end to a tumultuous season.

But for some reason the boys' smiles were muted. When one boy sidled up to me and whispered under his breath, "Yay, we're the seventeenth best team in the league," I saw exactly where his mind was. Then, story after story of similar expressions and I knew these boys were not satisfied; they expected way more of themselves, of their season.

I will say this.

I will say this with all candor in my mind, body, and soul. For our family, my son grew more as a basketball player in that year than any year he was coached by me. I admit that without any reservation and I credit his coach, Coach Applewhite.

Because of multiple injuries to the team's starting guards, my son was forced into action and matured as a player. I knew his strengths and weaknesses so I could flaunt or hide them as a game situation dictated. Coach Applewhite simply thrust Brock into action out of necessity, and he was forced to live or die on his own. And, in my opinion, Brock responded.

It taught us both a valuable lesson.

I was not the only coach who could make my son better. I needed to cut the apron strings. I was not some all-powerful and knowing basketball wizard. It was humbling. I am man enough to see that, know that, and respect that about his new coach. And I did respect his coach for that and do to this very day.

And my son gained confidence from being thrust into action. There was no plan B for the team. No hidden agenda. Due to multiple injured players, there was no one left on the bench. He had to play. He had to step up for his coach, his school, and his team.

And it was beautiful to witness. It didn't go perfectly. There were turnovers, missed shots, and dribbling mistakes, but that happens to everyone. And these were his own mistakes. He knew what they were; heck, he did them. By now he had that introspection built in. He knew what he needed to improve upon. This was no hiccup for my son, at all.

For my son, it was a year to remember.

SOMETIMES THE CLOTHES
DO MAKE THE MAN

When I was in sixth grade, a house on Sunnyside Avenue in Pleasantville where I grew up was called the Abbott House. It was a home for at-risk boys, mostly African American and Hispanic—the kind of place white families love in their old-growth, tree-lined suburban neighborhoods lined with Victorian homes.

One of my best friends at the time was Caleb David. Caleb lived two doors down from the Abbott House. Caleb's parents, ever the progressives (she an artist and he a psychiatrist), had already had their son over to the Abbott House multiple times to hang out with the boys who lived there. I came from the other side of town, equally modest, but more sheltered than Caleb.

Caleb's home and the Abbott House backed up to Pleasantville High School. Actually, to the Pleasantville High School exterior basketball courts—the kind built for all kinds of weather: stiff double rims, chain link nets for durability, and taut polls so tightly embedded in the asphalt to withstand the multiple vandals they knew would be climbing on them, hanging on them, and attempting their destruction after dark. Simply put, they weren't super friendly to a beginner's shot.

At times Caleb and I would be playing at his house and hear the kids from the Abbott House out there hooping. Caleb would turn to me and ask, "Wanna go play?"

"You mean, like, hoops with the brothers?"

"Yeah."

"You think we can?" I said half hoping he would say no.

"Sure."

And off we went. Caleb, all confident despite his small stature, and me, his big lummox of a sidekick, scared but wanting to play more than anything. I felt like I was entering the dragon's lair, playing hoops with the black kids. (Sounds way more racist as I write this today than I ever felt it as a child.)

I remember approaching for the first time. I was scared. Like really scared. Our family had been part of a church group that had the same boy come out of Harlem every summer to spend a few weeks with us. Tony was like another brother to me, special in every way, and he came for seven consecutive summers. So it wasn't the color of their skin that scared me. It was that I didn't think I could hang with them as a basketball player. And, I am fairly certain, they were thinking the same thing.

When we walked over, we saw them playing. Then they just stopped dribbling and stared at us. It was as if they heard a record scratch. Not sure if they were thinking *do not come over here, what's this*, or *now we about to kick some ass*, but it wasn't exactly the welcome wagon with warm cookies and local store coupons.

Caleb marched up like he belonged, and I trailed, shuffling along at a safe enough distance. I wanted to make certain I had enough of a head start if they got Caleb first.

"We got next, guys," Caleb exclaimed confidently.

After studying us up and down and making a few less than complimentary comments under their breath, they decided they might as well let us run with them. More bodies would make the game better, or so they must have thought.

Now, these kids were all on the verge of being men. They ranged from fifth grade to high school. Most always had their shirts off and were ripped, maybe a cigarette behind their ear as they played, long shorts, and cool sneakers—or so I thought. Each one had their own style. While they didn't have the money of these surrounding suburban households, they created their own style, and I remember thinking how cool it was as I played alongside them in my fuchsia, corduroy Ocean Pacific shorts that Mom got me at Bloomingdale's in White Plains.

What a pussy, they must have thought.

And we would play. We would play with kids like Leroy Triplet, Steven Young, Floyd James, David Thomas, and Pinky Sagittarius, who later ironically renamed himself Joaquin the Walking Joint.

True story, just ask Caleb.

I remember as the days progressed, as time progressed, as we got to know these guys, and I got better and better, the games became more fun and more relaxed. When just weeks before a teammate would look at you when they had the ball and intentionally not pass to you because you weren't deemed worthy in that nanosecond, I started to get passes returned. I started to be relied on to score. It started to become basketball. It's funny how a sport can break down barriers like that.

I always sought out those games.

And after the love of the game is established and your confidence builds, you start to look around and understand that your gear, your look, is equally as important. I'm not talking about the wannabes who can't play, and their parents buy them the most expensive sneakers (or OP shorts) year after year because that's what Jimmy wants.

I am talking about the real players who sweat and grind and have some skill. Who don't care about how many points they score, who are out there setting picks, grabbing boards, and playing D the way the game was intended to be played as a team—even if that team was only yours until the next pickup game got to eleven.

My style in the late seventies, early eighties was simple: white Nike high tops (there was only white in my day), double tube socks worn up to just below the knee, boxers that hung out of my Champion shorts, and a T-shirt, which was off half the time while playing shirts and skins. I am fairly certain the boxer idea came from one of the way cooler kids at the Abbott House.

My parents, for their part, hated my intentionally sloppy "boxer out" appearance. But to me, this was it. It fit my persona, a little sloppy, relaxed look, as if I wasn't trying as hard as I was actually trying. My friends from the Abbott House taught me that.

Anyway, the boxers became a big deal in our house.

My father wore tighty whiteys so I couldn't borrow his boxers, and my mom couldn't quite grasp this newfound rogue undergarment phenomenon of mine. She was simply not sure she wanted to invest in a three-pack of Hanes boxers if all the men in her family, heretofore, had been wearing tighty whiteys their whole life. This was a seismic shift in the natural order of her household, or at least its underwear drawers.

How would she wash them, fold them, care for them, these wayward boxers?

When she denied my first request for these seemingly taboo undergarments, I was undeterred and forced to improvise. I found an old pair of sweatpants. (I was the third boy in our house, so I lived on hand-me-downs for the first seventeen years of my life.) I took those old sweats and cut them with a scissors just above the knee. These were old sweats that had the string missing from the waistband, so I found a purple shoelace in my desk drawer, attached a safety pin to it, and pulled it through the waistband. That was some serious ingenuity for a suburban quasi-baller kid.

I slipped the sweats on and trimmed them further to what I thought would be the perfect length as I kept checking their length in the mirror over the dresser in my parents' bedroom.

My mom walked in and stared at me for a beat: "What are you doing?

"Making basketball shorts."

"You have a drawer full of basketball shorts."

"These are cooler."

"Cooler?"

"Yeah, you know, stylish," I said a little cocky.

"Stylish?"

"Yeah, stylish," I reiterated with a wry grin.

She just stared at me like, You idiot. "Why would you ruin a perfectly good pair of sweatpants?"

"Because you wouldn't buy me boxers," I shot back with more than a modicum of snark.

"This is a tighty whitey family!" she screamed as she stormed out of the room.

And as God as my witness, I did not get boxers. And as God as my further witness, I cut up two more pairs of old sweatpants. In fact, I soon lost my desire for boxers. I had created my own basketball undergarment and soon I started seeing other guys around school with cutoff sweatpants.

When a cool, local dad came up to me and said, "I knew you could play when I saw your cutoff sweatpants," it was all the external validation I needed. As if the swagger gods had confirmed my every suspicion.

And when I finally got the three pack of Hanes boxers as a Christmas stocking stuffer later that year, I had my mother return them because they held no allure to me now that I had created my own look.

8

HEMORRHOIDS

We parents screw it all up.

We think we know what's right for our kids, but really it's just our competitive nature that we inflict upon them and the games become ugly because of it. I indict myself in that.

At times I coach with the psychosis of Alex running down the hallways in *The Shining*. Not super attractive.

The thing about now heading into eighth grade was that the parents had become the most involved. At this point in their lives, the big question was where will these boys go to high school and what sports will they play?

Many of my team wish to play at the next level. Our school happens to be a feeder school to a large high school in the area known as Catholic. Our school is about 248 students made up of preschool through eighth grade. The freshman class at Catholic is 300, all boys. At Catholic, there are two freshman boys basketball teams made up of fifteen boys each.

The best athlete in our school made the team last year, but never played. To say it's competitive is an apocalyptic understatement. Last year athletes from Catholic went to Division 1 athletic programs like Notre Dame and the University of Washington, among others.

And most of our parents knew this.

All boys on our team have, or had, private trainers of some kind, and played on various AAU or select teams, all to get the maximum exposure and a little edge over the others. We all used to call each other and organize to play in AAU tournaments. By now everyone was off doing their own thing. Everyone needed to get that edge, to be the guy who makes it, to be THAT kid, to be one of the thirty.

It is a sad step each family must decide for themselves. It had now become every man for himself. The ugly part of getting older in competitive athletics.

My wife and I steadfastly reminded ourselves of the true talent level of our own kids and the joy we share not having traveled the club circuit to various remote locales on weekends, away from each other and their siblings.

Granted, we have driven to the local AAU tournaments twenty minutes away and disrupted entire weekends regularly, but, for our family, that is where we drew the line. Reno, Las Vegas, San Diego, LA, Oakland—these tournaments held no allure for us.

And why would they?

So we can tell our neighbors Jimmy's on the comp soccer team? Sure he is. I saw Jimmy kicking the ball around the 'hood. And guess what? Jimmy ain't no Messi, but you keep paying the two grand fee and eight hundred dollar weekend tourneys, hotels, and meals so Jimmy can play comp. I'll be home holding my son's hand, watching football with a cool drink in my hand and my feet up on the ottoman.

The allure of it all is the OxyContin-like addiction of hearing a club coach saying, "I'm seeing improvement in Jimmy, Mr. Meyer," when there truly is no long-term talent there. But those fateful words are what keeps us coming back. That keeps us paying. That keeps us addicted and in need of the methadone trip back to society when a "real" coach tells us Jimmy didn't make the squad. "Bu ... bu ... but his comp soccer coach said he had talent for the last four years."

Yup.

As a coach you see this day in and day out. As a coach you attempt to fight the insidiousness of the cancer that has spread through youth sports. I had a mother call me on the phone and break into tears when her child didn't make my team. She said they moved here and can't find coaches who teach fundamentals, explain strategy, and seemingly care about the kids. (I make sure he comes to our practices to learn more.) Together we lament how this has now become a huge business: personal trainers, AAU comp teams, skills training.

For what?

For a chance. A chance to dream. A chance that my child has some special gift. A gift that will make him succeed at the next level and perhaps beyond. What else are you gonna spend your money on, right?

I get it. I really do. We all love our kids and want to give them every opportunity we can. The most difficult part is truly listening to your adult brain and watching your child in practice, games, but, in my humble opinion, most importantly, when he is at home. What does he do? Does he go and pick up a basketball on his own and play? Does he watch endless basketball videos of the NBA highlights or theprofessorlive.com because he can't get the game out of his mind?

When I ask my son if he wants to play at the next level, he shrugs his shoulder. "I don't really care, Dad."

And I genuinely don't think he does.

Do I want him to?

I played in high school and I loved it. I believe it taught me so much about life and people. Your role on a team. Working together toward a common goal. Having success and failure. Seeing what people were made of. All the amazing lessons sports teach us.

But my school was a tiny public school with 500 kids combined (about fifty or sixty boys per grade) in the small school (Class C) division of suburban New York State athletics.

My son is headed to a high school where athletes are now recruited. Yes, recruited. Maybe not overtly like college athletes with the lure of free tuition, room, board, and whatever else. But covertly, or as they justify, based on "financial need." High schools need to be competitive too.

But, for our family, I know it is not truly him. My son still enjoys being tucked in at night. My son who, as recently as last summer, would fall asleep in his ten-year-old brother's bed because they were talking and they truly are best friends.

See, in my mind's eye, I know this other side of my son that the outside world doesn't see. That I don't care for them to see. Because this is ours. Our family. How we believe in family above all. How we will always place family above all. Because that is what is the most important thing to us in this world. That is what his mother and I preach to them daily. That is our sustenance, our energy drink of life. How his courtside immaturity is somehow lauded at home because his mother and I know the love of this child and his relationship with his brothers is light-years more important to us than any number of points, assists, or rebounds he will ever record on some random stat sheet that once the page is turned that evening will, most likely, never be seen again.

And how additionally, the love of, and for, his parents and brothers will last a lifetime. That will matter a hundredfold more to us than his making a basketball team in high school. And that love, however altruistic in his parents' minds, is what we strive for more than anything else in this world. It's all we really want.

And I know, I know I can hear you say, if he had that kind of talent, that big school talent, I would feed that beast as many parents do.

Absolutely.

Just saying I have seen more rec league talented kids getting pushed to achieve their parents' dreams of trying to play at the next level even when that next level is not there for most of us. I knew very early on that I had rec league talented kids. They had a rec league talented dad.

I hold no true aspiration of any of my sons playing at the next level. And they have showed me no true desire to play at the next level despite being exposed to leagues, coaches, and trainers. Heck, I even built a frickin' hoop court in our backyard.

Listen to your kids. Listen to your kids' words, watch their actions, study their responses and behavior. You know your child. Maybe it's not for them.

My kids love video games, hosing down and soaping up their trampoline and slip-sliding around on it, playing hide-n-seek and football in the front yard, swimming, watching YouTube on their iPad, trading basketball and baseball cards, and watching sports with their dad, among other things.

They just like being kids.

Each of us parents has a different motivation. Our past lives, our current lives, including our jobs, our love relationships, our friends, our hopes and dreams, desires and our needs all have a profound impact on how we motivate our children, how we provide for them.

I have witnessed so many children just going through the motions, being shuttled from one game to the other, their bodies breaking down, their interest waning because how do you get up for your fourth game in a weekend in a gym filled with twelve courts and hundreds of kids playing all around you again, and again, and again, and again?

For the plastic medal affixed with the red, white, and blue ribbon?

I have seen it.

No, I have *done* it—and still do it. No, this is a puppy mill with real live children. This is not what I remember.

Where is that special feeling of putting it all on the line for that one special game a week? That do-or-die situation at 10:00 a.m. in the high school gym and my excitement, nay nervousness, in being able to play on the same hardwood as Rich Pearson, Jeff Ogren, Mark and John Rookwood, and John Cavalleri of the Pleasantville Panthers High School varsity team?

Holy crap. You mean, I get to play on the same court as them?

That was excitement. One game a week. One practice. An eight-game recreation season against my friends from our school.

Heaven.

And this is not some sanctimonious coach spouting his pious opinions. Again, I am no better. I am just as guilty. I am guilty of letting my third grader play in AAU tournaments and absolutely going ballistic on the sideline as we pressed the ever living shit out of teams who could barely get the ball in bounds to their point guard.

Yes, I was that guy. Still am. Maybe a little wiser, a few more gray hairs, fatter gut, maybe mellowed. Maybe not.

I'll tell you when the season's over.

SYMPATHY FOR THE DEVIL

It was seventh grade. We all heard there was a new family coming to our school. We all heard they could ball. The kid in our grade was a point guard. We heard he could hit bombs. He had two younger brothers who were ballers too. They instantly became the best players in all their grades. It was a massive upgrade to the village of Pleasantville basketball, let alone our middle school team.

He was a transfer student of the best kind. A kid who could take your squad to the next level by simply enrolling. Older. Like one of those kids who comes from another town and the parents hold him back because he is immature or to get a leg up.

These were leg-up people.

These were the Ceislers. Three boys, all big-time scorers. They *were* basketball. They transferred from Scarsdale and brought their family love of hoop to our town. And it was infectious.

The dad was a real wheeler and dealer businessman in a variety of ventures. He knew whom to connect with to get his boys the upper hand on all basketball teams. He immediately found our gym teacher, Coach B, and made fast friends. He knew how to start the conversation. His boys would ultimately have to prove themselves, but you go straight to the source. This was low-stakes basketball, so no money was exchanged, but a few lunches and kind words were just as effective in this arena.

The mom, Alice, was a frickin' rock star. She knew the game better than most coaches at this level, and certainly more than I did. She was brimstone and hellfire on the sideline. You could hear her as you sped by her seat in the stands. You could see her screaming at the refs, her epiglottis rattling. She was no joke!

And after the game, her voice would miraculously change to a softer maternal tone and she would always find you for a well-appointed compliment. It was obvious she saw everything. She would mention the smallest things like a pick for her son in the second half of the third quarter from the right foul line extended when he hit that bomb or how you dove for a loose ball in front of the opposing bench at the 3:37 mark of the second quarter.

Her compliments were genuine and well-placed to illicit the necessary dirty work she knew she needed to get her boys open looks at the rim. In many ways I think she saw me as a necessary piece of that ultimate puzzle. And her compliments were hardwood gold—all I really needed to keep doing that dirty work. For me, it was as if Pat Summitt herself was speaking to me.

I instantly knew this was a family I wanted to be near. They were basketball. That's all they cared about. That's all they lived for. That's what they did. Nothing like my family. No, this was a true hoop family, and I wanted to be close to it.

Their arrival in our school district was the perfect confluence of my budding love of the game and me transitioning to playing it more regularly. They were instrumental, if not pivotal, in pouring more gunpowder on that spark.

The guy in my class was Brad.

For Pleasantville area basketball, Brad could play. He had a jump shot when jump shots were scarce. Ya know, the first kid who had a halfway decent jump shot at this age and was always the leading scorer. This guy had that shot, but what he had way more than his good shot was his complete and utter disregard for a conscience about that shot. He would rip from anywhere and everywhere, and he didn't care what you, yo' momma, the coach, the principal, or the mayor thought of it either.

And therein lay his greatness ... and his infamy. Other kids didn't like him because he would just rip it from anywhere, at any time. Every town, every league, everyone has a Brad on their team at some point.

But for me, I loved it.

Why?

I liked winning and I knew I couldn't hit those bombs.

You see, my true gift as a player was my realization, and I had it from a very early age.

I knew I was not the best. I knew I wasn't even among the best in my class. I genuinely knew that at this age. And yet it did not deter me, not even once. That's how I could tell it was love. I knew my shot was not as good as the best players'; I knew I couldn't dribble like they could; I knew I didn't have the court vision of the guy who brought the ball up. I knew all that early on.

But being the youngest in a family of five, I also knew how to observe the landscape and fit in.

I knew what made the best kids happy. I knew they wanted to shoot. No, I knew they were addicted to shooting like a skid row drug addict is addicted to meth. And I knew they couldn't stop that addiction of checking how many points they scored in the scorebook at the end of each and every game. I saw them do it as if that was their validator of greatness.

So I just freed them. I freed them so they could score more.

I would set pick after pick and block their defender time and time again. Big kids, little kids, fat kids, slow kids, and I knew it was working because the defenders were pissed at me time and time again. And in games when they couldn't push me and get away with it like the older kids did in local pickup games, I would hear the screams from their disgruntled teammates, "Call out the frickin' pick!" And I loved to hear those words. That was my joy, my validator of a job well done.

I knew what scorers wanted, and I fulfilled my role.

And, oh, how I benefited. Because I knew I would be feeding off Brad's scraps, his misses, and I also knew there would be plenty. I saw that firsthand. All I had to do was crash the boards and get after it. I was the remora to the scoring shark that was Brad. His misses turned into easy lay-ups, put-backs, and garbage points for me. The garbage were the missed shots that I put back in for easy lay-ups.

I fed off that garbage. So much so my coach, Coach Bergholtz, actually called me the garbage man. I took no offense to the moniker. I knew my station in life and I loved it. I loved me some garbage.

Then, as we started to play together and Brad saw how hard I was working, he also started firing passes my way.

And that's when it started to get really good.

So then I found myself wanting to be at the Ceisler house as much as I could because I knew they would always find the next game.

And that's the other thing the Ceislers taught me—that basketball was not just a winter sport. They found leagues in the summer where we played with way better competition. Today this is commonplace with AAU, comp leagues, and traveling teams, but back in the early eighties this was unknown to most people.

At first, I was not always asked to join them. They would go to bigger towns to play with better competition with friends of theirs from outside our school district. The idea was that you would want to roll into these gyms with your best team so you would cherry-pick your team of ballers. At this time, I was not one of the ballers. I was the extra body whenever they were short or needed another guy. And a willing body at that. But I didn't always get the call.

And that made me want it even more. I knew they didn't think I was good enough and that pissed me off. Like when you call someone on the phone and ask them to play and you can hear in their voice they don't want to play with you, that they're dodging you. Yeah, that happened a bunch.

But it only fueled the fire. I would work harder and say to myself, "I'll show you and your perfect little basketball family replete with mother who knows more about the game than John Wooden. I'll show you!"

And as I improved, I got the call more regularly. I knew they were playing with older kids, black kids, rougher kids, faster kids, bigger kids, stronger kids, better kids, and I wanted in. But they only let me in so far. They determined the teams, and I wasn't fully in that crowd yet. I asked. I asked a lot.

And when I ultimately got the call to join them, first, I sat on the pines dreaming about going in, watching the opposing players' strengths and weaknesses, knowing what I would do when, and if, I got in. I studied the game. And when I got in, I knew what they wanted. Set a pick, free the scorer, crash the boards, and try not to turn the ball over.

Slowly, over time, I started getting more and more opportunities, putting rebounds back up and getting swatted into the third row, then learning a pump fake, and how to use my body, my ass. I had a Kardashian-ass before a Kardashian-ass was all the rage.

And here's how the years went: Before my freshman year, I was occasionally called and had sporadic playing time. Before my sophomore year, I was called and played. Before my junior year, I was the sixth man and occasional starter. Before my senior year, I played all the time.

I loved the atmosphere. I loved it all: the un-airconditioned gyms, the sweat, the drive to and from a gym in all the different towns talking basketball the whole way. I loved rollin' into a gym with your crew and sussin' up the competition; I felt like such a bad-ass rollin' into a gym with my boys. I loved everything about it. I craved the run. It truly was love, and "the family" made it so.

THERE'S WALDO

My parents never came to these summer league games.

They were starting a new business (my father's civil engineering firm) out of our home and had that stress. I had so much freedom because they were too busy trying to get that business off the ground. In fact, my parents never pushed me once to play any sport, not once. They simply said yes or okay when I asked to go play ball.

My father played no part, zero, in any of my sports insanity, and I turned out fine. You see, some kids are okay with their fathers not being at every game, at every practice, pushing them to do sports. Some kids are just fine. I look back and think about the question everyone wants to ask: Did you miss your father being a part of this life?

I can honestly say with all candor that I did not.

I know this must sound strange, but I didn't. See, as a third child and, in my case, a third son, you observe. You shut your mouth and observe your parents, your older brothers, the family dynamic, and you get to understand the dynamics at an early age. And, as such, I knew who my father was.

He was a businessman. He loved it. You could see that on his face when he talked about his work, the way he talked about his work. He laughed when he told stories about it; he smiled a true, genuine smile; you could literally see it in his eyes. I could see he had his own thing building this business out of our home with people milling about the makeshift desks set up in our living room and den, sharing Mom's home-cooked meals with men and women who were moonlighting for my father to help him build his own dream—and maybe make a few extra bucks along the way.

I expected nothing from my father in sports except to maybe come to a big game. And he did. He always did. But to me, even when he did, he always somehow seemed out of place. Like spotting Waldo in the picture books. I could always see him sticking out in the crowd, sans the red and white striped hat.

See, he grew up as a student and a worker bee in his immigrant father's ice cream parlor in the Bronx. He went to the Bronx High School of Science. He was smart and he knew how to work. That was what his German heritage was bred for. That's what he was good at. That's where he thrived. That's what he enjoyed. And I harbored zero resentment of him for doing what he loved—I still don't.

And in some strange way, I think he silently respected that I went off and did this all on my own. No prodding. No help. No encouragement to speak of. Starting quarterback, forward, and shortstop and captain of all three high school teams begat from a man who could barely hold a Wiffle ball bat.

I think we silently respected each other.

And now. Now I am grateful he worked his ass off because he provided the most amazing life for all of us, all five of our families, and taught me so much about business and people and hard work and the importance of loving what you do for a living. "You love what you do, and you will never work a day in your life" is how the saying goes. He loved what he did and made a career out of it.

That is vital for living.

So, you see, sometimes parents don't need to push at all. I think we can all learn a heck of a lot from my father. Let your child find the joy they want, not the joy you want.

10

DROPPING THE HAMMER
... ON MY FOOT

Our league hosts a summer basketball league for incoming varsity (seventh and eighth grade) competitive teams. It is a quick eight-game schedule in June and July so teams can assess what they've got for the upcoming season.

I am currently NOT the varsity comp coach at my son's school. Coach Applewhite is.

After our sons' less than stellar seventh grade season, Tim's Dad, Coach Quincy and I went in and asked our Athletic Director if we could coach the boys next year. We indicated the rest of the seventh-grade families were behind us. Our AD said he would "consider" our request.

While I was pleased with his "consideration," I was surprised he didn't give us the position on the spot. We thought he, like us, was not pleased with last season's performance, but there was obviously a school protocol he needed to follow and an administration with whom he needed to consult before rendering his decision.

That made me uneasy.

Then, at the end of the seventh-grade school year, with summer league about to begin, Coach Applewhite declined to coach the summer league team. He said he wanted to spend more time with his family. So our AD gave Coach Quincy and me the job.

Up until a week before summer league started, Coach Quincy and I had thought it was our team. We never even knew Coach Applewhite was being considered for the summer league post. His official decline caused more alarms to go off in my head. I knew he was still being considered for coaching the boys this winter.

Coach Quincy and I were, however, thrilled. We would finally be back with the team. It's all we had talked about since enduring the pain of last season from the sidelines. Plus, we enjoyed being together as dads, coaching our sons. We had always assumed the summer league would be made up of the same boys we were considering for that upcoming season. We thought we would be able to cherry-pick the exact team we wanted. But then our AD sent out an email to ALL of the boys in seventh and eighth grade; it was a school team after all.

When twelve kids signed up, we lobbied for two teams. But, in our hearts, we knew that wasn't realistic with everyone's summer vacations and busy schedules. We knew there would always be boys missing games, including our own.

Then, a final proviso from our AD that arrived as pleasantly as a throat punch from MMA's McGregor:

"And I want everyone to play equally. I want it to be fun."

The kiss of death for a competitive team heading into eighth grade.

I knew we were in trouble.

This equal play time has never been our team's thing. We had a very competitive nucleus and a plethora of equally competitive parent opinions on speed dial. This was like an AAU team only all these boys happened to be from the same school. Our boys knew, early on, you earn your playing time. We made that abundantly clear to each and every one. Each boy knew he would be given a fair shake, and he could start if he worked in practice and if he was better than the kid next to him or otherwise brought some intangible we were looking for (picks, hustle, defense).

There were no favorites. It was sometimes especially brutal for me as I looked down at the end of the bench and saw my own fifth grader looking back at me holding up his arms, as if to say, "Put me in the frickin' game!" But I couldn't, not when I had The Rocket playing in front of him, a whip-fast sixth grader who was clearly better than he in every facet of the game. That happens too in life.

Did it hurt?

Of course it did.

It hurt me at the base of my soul. I had to go home with my son and hear his cries at night of why he wasn't playing as much as the other kids. I took those moments to be valuable teaching lessons to encourage him to practice and get better. Lessons, I feel, he took to heart and made him the player he is today.

I am so abundantly proud of him for that.

To further complicate things is this: If you truly know me, you would know that I am a sensitive man, a soft and squishy dad. The type of man who probably babies his sons too much. I know that, I intellectualize that, and yet I still do it. I figure the world is harsh enough, and they will find that out on their own soon enough one day. If it's a few years later than most kids, I'm okay with that. I am flawed that way.

But I won't play my son over a kid who is clearly better. That's just ugly.

MY FIRST REUNION with the boys since March of their sixth-grade year was this summer league after their seventh-grade year, some fifteen months since last coaching them.

When I got them back in summer league, they were now thirteen going on fourteen, far removed from those attentive eleven- and twelve-year-olds I had previously coached.

The differences in the boys' minds at these two ages was night and day.

What was so great about our sixth-grade year is that the boys actually listened. They were mostly twelve years old when testosterone was merely a faint glimmer on the horizon, and it had not yet made its epic journey through their bodies. They still saw me as their coach, an authority figure, a dad who had been with them since their youth. They never questioned anything when we implemented something new, or crazy, or decided to press or not press. Whatever I threw at them, they were game. There was always an implicit trust there.

And we were winning; everyone is happy when you're winning. When we ultimately lost the only game we did that year, there were, of course, rumblings, and they always pointed to the coach: "He's just a dad." "He's not a basketball coach." All the normal things people say when you don't achieve what is expected.

And yes, it's the parents. The boys don't think like that. The boys love what we had. They knew Coach Quincy, Coach Roger, and I quite well by then. They knew we told them how it was. We were tough, but fair, and we would give them everything we got each and every practice and game. Everything!

Children can see that passion. Children feed off that passion. Children get excited off that passion.

And the parents for the most part are awesome. But they are also not there. They are not in that gym day in and day out. They are not witnessing practice. They are not seeing their son zoning in and out of relative consciousness, not able to focus or understand basic concepts. Turning the ball over and over, not being prepared. They just think Johnny is a rock star because they begat Johnny from their womb and seed and how could Johnny not be awesome in every way, shape, and form.

No, ours was a unique journey. When you are in a gym with a child from kindergarten through eighth grade, you know how his day went, how is week is going, how school is going, how his friendships are going, what his competitive nature truly is. Parents don't see that.

They see Johnny at home in his pj's eating spaghetti and maybe grunting a few words about his day. Ours—coach and player—is a truly unique perspective.

A coach in many instances is safer to talk to than a parent. And as such there is an immeasurable amount of responsibility to these children. You must know when to challenge them and when to lay off. How hard to push and how to just listen. To be an amateur psychologist of sorts really.

And as a coach, you need to make mistakes too. Sometimes too harsh, sometimes too soft. That is why another dad (er, assistant) is always vital. In my case, I have two of the best. Coach Quincy (Tim's dad) is a student of the kids, and Coach Roger (Stevie's dad) the strategist. (Coach Roger had obligations with his daughter in the summer so he was not with us.)

So as we began this summer, almost in their final year of middle school, we started to see some of the boys have their own agendas and their personalities were changing too. They weren't all as unified as they once were. There were slight divisions in the friendships, less passing going on, and they weren't as tight-knit a group as they were two years ago.

It's called growing up.

It was clear to me that my coaching style had to change. In the heat of a summer game one of my players told me, "That won't work," then took the erasable pen out of my hand to draw his own play on my basketball board. I almost crapped my pants. I was so taken aback, I did all I could do not to rip him a new one right there in front of his teammates. I bit my tongue and smiled before sending them back on the floor to "RUN THE FREAKIN' PRESS I JUST TOLD YOU TO RUN, ONLY RUN IT RIGHT THIS TIME!"

As they broke the huddle, I looked at Coach Quincy and said, "This is gonna be a very different season."

Were these boys now that audacious? Had their parents already gotten into their heads that it's time to start thinking about making your high school team? Coach Meyer is just a dad. We gotta get ready for the "real coaches"?

This was going to be tough. This wasn't sixth-grade coaching. These weren't little kids anymore. These boys were becoming men. Coach Meyer didn't hold the same allure as he used to. I had to find a new way. I had to change. I had to determine what motivated them now.

In most instances, coaches coach the same age group year after year. In doing so, you know what kids of that exact age group are prepared to learn and what you as a coach can expect of them.

I'm just a dad following his son and his friends through their lives. I was the one who had to notice these subtle changes in their personalities as they matured and grew. I needed to adapt. These little boys from kindergarten were ready for something new.

I needed to change.

We did as our AD suggested.

We played everyone equally, and we lost our first game to our crosstown rivals, St. Maximilian Kolbe. We had beaten them four times in sixth grade, but they ended up winning it all when we were upset in the semis. I still knew we were better than they were. So this was an upset. They came to play and put the throttle down. We played everyone "equally"—and lost.

The next day at work my phone rang. Could I jump on a conference call, and would I mind waiting as two parents conferenced me in?

Ahhh, sure?

Then, it started—

"What the fuck was that? That was total bullshit!" They jumped down my throat. "We have to play every kid equally? Really? What the hell is this rec league bullshit?"

"I know," I said.

And it went on. And I held the phone away from my ear like you see in the movies when someone is getting chewed out. And the beating went on for what seemed like forever.

"I know, I know. I am just doing what I am told."

"If that's the way it's gonna be, why are we even playing?"

And you can imagine how it went back and forth from there. The problem is that I see both sides clearly. There are not enough boys for two teams. You want everyone who signs up to play. It's a school spirit thing and our school needs to do that for everyone—equally. After all, it's *just* summer league. But then there are those parents who know what we have been through, our unique journey. Those who have a shared singular vision for their child playing at the highest level he is capable of playing for their school. This was not that. They knew that and I knew that.

My job was to navigate the summer league with a team that was used to playing on the merits, at all costs, and who didn't understand, or want to understand, the play equal concept, which was the directive from our athletic director.

And to make matters worse is that I was only being "considered" for the coaching job for this winter. If I screwed this up and offended the AD of our school, I was out. I was keenly aware of my predicament.

So we continued to play everyone equally. As my core players would be replaced by kids who were not as advanced, they'd jog off the court and say, "Why you taking me out, Coach?" This happened on more than twenty occasions. They knew what was happening and made sure their displeasure was duly noted.

I explained to them that this was a school rule. To a child, they guffawed under their breath as you can only imagine.

The next time we played our archrivals a few weeks later, I had this conference call in my mind, the AD's directive in my head, and my players reminding me, "We're going all out this time, right?" Couple that with a few subtle stares from the crowd and a friendly slap on the back, "Let's drop the hammer, Coach," and we're off.

Now I was playing to win.

We were in one of those otherworldly grooves at the end of the first half pressing, getting turnovers, bumpin' three after three in a flurry of seconds, when their coach wisely sensed the game getting out of hand and called a time-out.

As our team ran back to our huddle, Coach Quincy reminded me, "We gotta get the other boys in." So now, up fourteen, loving what I was seeing and rushing before the buzzer sounded to end the time-out, I placed the entire second team in the game. (In retrospect, unfair and stupid. I should have slowly mixed them in with others.)

By the time the second half buzzer sounded, less than two minutes later, the second unit had given up the entire lead. When they got back to the bench at halftime, I leaned into them:

"You cannot do that! You simply cannot do that! We cannot practice during the week, learn all that we learn, and then you come out here and do that." Only in way more colorful language at a way higher decibel level.

I saw they were upset. I was too harsh. This was summer league, ya know, for fun.

We ended up winning and did not play the kids equally. It was a gratifying win. I got the nods from the usual suspects, and we headed out of the gym. I was proud of the boys and the way they played. But I also had an uneasy feeling. I knew I didn't play everyone per the AD's rules, and I knew I was too harsh with that second unit.

The next day, I got a call from Coach Quincy. He started off by reiterating it was a good victory and we needed to do it. To make sure our rivals didn't go into the fall knowing they beat us twice in the summer. It was psychological warfare. I said I felt bad the other kids didn't play as much. Coach Quincy wanted to win as bad as I did, but then he said, "Yeah, Grandpa wasn't too happy."

I knew exactly who he was talking about.

Last year we got two brothers in our class. They were the estranged sons of a former professional baseball player. At this time, they were not currently speaking to their dad. To say they came with a lot of emotional sensitivity is a colossal understatement.

Their grandparents played an unbelievable role in their grandchildren's lives. Like what real families do. True families. Their grandfather was a former career baseball coach and a good one from what I heard. He must've heard my tirade from across the gym and, on the way out after the game, told Coach Quincy, "A coach should never talk to kids that way."

And he was right.

When Coach Quincy told me this on the phone, I was embarrassed. We hung up the phone, and I thought about the situation for about a half an hour.

It bothered me.

I was that asshole who forgot about the various skill levels and personalities of each of the "children" on our team and the "fun" we were supposed to be having in summer league.

I was that guy.

I quickly wrote Grandpa, his wife, and their daughter (the boys' mom) an email and cc'd Coach Quincy, apologizing for my behavior.

Grandpa responded almost immediately and suggested he come by my office to talk.

My office? Like, where I work?

I agreed, and we did. Coach Quincy, myself, and Grandpa, the former coach. The real coach. The guy who now taught coaching clinics to children about the value of sports and sportsmanship. I asked if he wanted to use me as the example of how not to coach.

He smiled and was gracious, but inside I could see him thinking, *I don't want you near my classes.*

We met for over an hour, and he educated us, not in any pompous, holier-than-thou manner, but in a kind, constructive, and understanding one. He made all solid points, and Coach Quincy and I tried to explain the pressure from the parents, our kids' expectations, our archrivals, all the normal excuses a coach would come up with to try and rationalize his poor behavior.

He smiled the smile of twenty Buddhas. Like, you mere mortals shall understand one day.

Coach made a huge impression on me that day. He gave me a coaching pamphlet and a Pulitzer Prize–winning book on coaching, a less-than-subtle gesture.

I was grateful for the counsel he provided me that day.

Thank you, Coach.

11

41 HILLVIEW DRIVE

We lived in a modest house perched on top of a hill. Its lawn and shrubs were kept immaculate by our gardener (my grandfather) who loved to do those types of tasks. The garage was similarly set at the pinnacle of the hill. In the winters, our father made his three sons get up early and shovel the snow off the driveway so he could get to work.

We would open the garage, take a snow shovel off the wall, point it down the driveway, and slide, generally, the entire way down the asphalt pitch as the snow was cleared from our shovels until we got to the bottom of the driveway at the street. There, the town's snowplows did their job of clearing the public streets, but their plows pushed mounds of snow onto the bottom of each driveway, blocking their egress. This is where the muscle of three sons was needed to get Dad's car out. As I dug out the snow, I looked over by the mailbox.

I knew the spot.

That Christmas of 1978, I wanted an actual basketball hoop of my own in the worst way. I begged my parents. I begged them to put it in. I even begged them months before. I said I would dig the hole. It's all I wanted. Just my own hoop, nothing else.

I woke up Christmas morning with the joy of ten grandparents at the birth of their first grandchild to find—nada! In my parents' defense, tons of wrapped presents, but no hoop. How do you put a basketball hoop, backboard, and pole under the tree, is what "Santa" said.

Fat bastard, I thought to myself.

My older brother was going off to college that August. He had begrudgingly thrown an endless series of pop flies and grounders to (and at) me in the front yard for the greater part of our childhood.

He did a lot.

When he went to college, I needed something to keep me busy. My parents knew that. My middle brother and father didn't enjoy athletics like we did; my older brother was my sports soul mate growing up despite our four-year age gap.

So in the spring, when the snow melted, my plan was strategically hatched. I chose the exact spot I had eyed the previous winter. Our mailbox sat at the bottom of the driveway on the right. Sure, there was a three-inch curb delineating the street from our property that might have dissuaded a more prudent child for fear of breaking his ankle on every lay-up, but I knew exactly where it could work.

And then they did it.

They bought a metal pole. My grandfather and I affixed a backboard to it. We checked our *Encyclopedia Britannica* for heights. We dug a hole on our property a few inches in from the curb, put the pole in it so the hoop hung over onto the street, leveled it, dumped a bag of concrete and some water in, and viola, I had my own hoop. I remember looking at it almost crying. My grandfather made me wait a few days for the concrete to dry. Heck, I waited fourteen years, what was another few days.

Now Hillview Drive was higher in the middle of the street, sloping ever so slightly to the curb. It was designed as such for proper street water runoff. Thus, my ten-foot regulation rim was a slightly easier shot from the foul line due to the slight concave shape of the street. But I didn't care. It was a hoop. My hoop. At the bottom of my driveway. And anyway this design flaw made me have greater home field advantage in all tête–à–têtes that were envisioned here.

Now I could play any time I wanted to, any day, in any type of weather, whenever I wanted, all day if I wanted. This was love to me at fourteen years old. This was exactly what I wanted.

And I shot. I shot endlessly.

Next to the castle for my army men I received as a five-year-old, my basketball hoop was the greatest gift I had ever received.

That hoop became my salvation. I played with friends, neighborhood kids, a little one-on-one here, a few two-on-twos there; three-on-threes felt like the mosh pit at a Nirvana concert.

But nothing was as fun as simply imagining the various scenarios in my head and playing them out in real time. There were the buzzer beaters that everyone practices: "3-2-1" and shoot as the ball flies to win or lose a do-or-die game, doing a George "The Iceman" Gervin finger roll from ten feet out or Kareem skyhook from somewhere in the middle of the lane, and of course trying to dunk. The endless attempts to obtain proper lift only to be weighed down by the limits of my natural abilities. It is the same scenario repeated by children the world over wherever they hoop—only the idols' names have changed.

Of course, I had heard the stories of Larry Bird shooting endlessly in his hometown of French Lick, Indiana. His shot allegedly became what it was because of his endless, repetitive shooting alone in his yard, only he truly knows the stories that enabled an unheard-of kid from Indiana State to find greatness. For me, like many boys and girls I am certain, his epic battle with Magic Johnson in the NCAA college basketball finals in 1979 only fueled my personal fire. A battle that would usher in a new era in NBA basketball with the advent of the three-point line.

The NBA instituted the three-point line for the 1979–1980 season. That was Magic Johnson and Larry Bird's rookie year in the NBA.

Some speculate the NBA adopted it for Larry Bird. To give more finesse players a fighting chance. Who knew, over time, that it would change the way the game was played.

Heretofore, the NBA was a slow transition game because that's how general managers had built their traditional teams since the inception of basketball. Fast guys dribble up the court, feed big guys in the post. It was a center-dominated game. Now, with the three-point line, you could slowly see where the game was headed. It was a brilliant marketing move by then commissioner David Stern and his team. It created more excitement and built the future of the NBA around the two electric personalities of Magic and Bird.

First there were only a few, like Bird, who could drain it from afar, which then ushered in the three-point shooting specialists like Steve Kerr, Dell Curry, then Reggie Miller and Ray Allen, until finally the all-out, long-range warfare of today, in which not only guards like Harden, Curry, and Klay Thompson drain it, but now 7-foot 260-pound big men like Joel Embiid, Anthony Davis, or Karl-Anthony Towns can fill it from deep.

In many ways my life and love of basketball has mirrored the ascent of the NBA from a childhood love of Dr. J in the American Basketball Association (the league that *originally* utilized the three-point line to add excitement to its game) to its trajectory of the NBA worldwide today.

But, honestly, the three-point line held no allure to me personally because, as I mentioned, I knew I was not that guy. I never wanted to be Larry Bird, or Magic Johnson for that matter. I always liked guys who were my body type, guys like Mark Aguirre, formerly of DePaul University and its legendary Coach Ray Meyer, and Charles Barkley of Auburn, guys who were undersized but would hustle and pound around the rim.

So, while I knew that three-point line was there, I simply practiced lay-ups, foul shots, and a series of lost post moves and midrange jumpers mimicking my heroes.

My own hoop gave me a great deal of "me" time and provided me with the perfect release to let my mind run. It was unlike football and baseball for me because I could practice alone and get better. Theoretically, in those other sports, you needed another person in order to practice. And I found a solitary beauty in shooting alone. It became a very zen place for me.

I loved that hoop.

And there was really nothing special about it. A metal pole in the ground, a few bags of concrete, a backboard, rim, a net, and a ball. That was it. So simple, yet it provided me so much joy. This is where my love of basketball grew even greater. Where I honed my game, where I got better. Where I could step outside my door and work at improving. The driveway hoop made it easier, more convenient, more personal. That time spent at the bottom of my driveway shooting baskets was among my most cherished childhood memories. I could see myself getting better. I could feel it.

How would I know at age fourteen that basketball would become such a large part of the fabric of my life? How could anyone foreshadow this? What drives a man? Where do we all find our joy? How a simple game, and a boy's love of it, grew into a family's obsession, while, at the same time, fully understanding none of us will ever become professional basketball players.

It's so simple.

Throw a 29.5-inch leather, round, brown ball into a 45-cm round rim, ten feet high in the air.

Oh, the absurdity of its creator.

Oh, the madness.

Oh, the brilliance.

I am but a small, young man. But I can see its brilliance.

THE DROUGHT ENDS

I remember it distinctly.

I remember the day.

I was maybe fifteen at this time, he maybe nineteen. Up to this point in my life, I was the sycophant always begging him to play with me at every turn. Of course he did (as only a firstborn knows how to), when he felt like it

Funny how you remember things.

No, this day, this was different. On this day, my older brother came to me. He saw me shooting *on my court* and came to me. It started fairly innocently just feeding each other after every made shot and, when we missed, giving the other a bounce pass for one last lay-up and then the other guy feeds you until you miss and repeat—ya know, basic basketball etiquette.

After a while I said, "You wanna go?"

He stared at me for a beat. I saw the look in his eyes. I saw what he was thinking in that instant. Can I still take him?

"Sure." He smiled back at me.

But this was no ordinary game.

This was a game to twenty-one, brotha a brotha, in a game that had now become my own. (He never played basketball in high school, sticking to the two sports he excelled at, football and baseball. And he was great at both.)

I knew that.

I knew where his vulnerability lay. That, and now as a fifteen-year-old heading into my sophomore year, my body type was different than his. It is sometimes shocking to see your sibling come home from college and they are smaller than you when, previously, your whole life they had been this larger-than-life figure. I had hit my growth spurt while he was gone, and now I was taller and thicker than his smaller and scrappier frame.

I didn't care. I didn't care one bit. I wanted to win. And with my newly arrived hormones pumpin' through my body, I was gonna do anything, and everything, to beat his ass.

I backed him down under that rim and scored lay-up after lay-up, turn around after turnaround, and there was not a frickin' thing he could do about it. Sure he could foul me, but we both knew. We both knew as the game was progressing what was happening. A seismic shift in the natural order of things in our household.

And I loved it. I loved it right up until the last shot for the win, in which, at this time, he wasn't even playing defense. He had given up.

And when it was over, like only an older brother can do, he said nothing, picked up his shirt, and went back inside our childhood home.

I stayed there for a minute and just kept shooting. No, I stayed there for a long while and just kept shooting. I thought about what had just happened. And unless you're a younger sibling of a highly competitive older brother or sister, you may not truly be able to fully comprehend this, but, you see, I had never done this. I had never beaten my older brother. At anything. Ever. In my entire life. Not checkers, Monopoly, badminton, Risk, jacks, lawn darts, tennis, Parcheesi, nothing! He wouldn't let it happen. He seemingly just willed every victory to happen. Like 8,462,333–0, fifteen years and 0.

But now, on my court, I had beaten my older brother at something.

A seminal moment in growing up.

At the dinner table later that night my mom's sixth sense kicked in. She knew the house felt different. You could feel it. She could feel it.

"What happened out there?" she asked.

"I won."

She turned from the hot stove and looked right at me.

I W-O-N, I articulated it more succinctly and more pronounced.

I saw the look on her face. By now, as a child, you know when things shock your mother. She knew about his 8,462,333–0 record. This, my victory, shocked my mother too. She almost laughed.

"I finally frickin' beat him," I said beaming.

She turned back to the stove and finished cooking the sloppy joes. But I could see the corners of her cheeks rise. She was smiling. I think she had been quietly rooting for me all along. She liked the underdog.

I'll never forget my hoop on Hillview Drive. It is where the imagination of my Nerf basketball court in my boyhood bedroom transitioned to my own actual hoop in the outside world.

My basketball hoop at 41 Hillview Drive in Pleasantville, New York. Oh, the memories.

12

CHRISTMAS IN OCTOBER

The start of their eighth-grade school year begins with flag football. It is a short season, five league games, followed by potentially three playoff games ending on the first weekend of November. The following Monday, basketball begins.

Flag football is, in many ways, a harbinger of what is to come in basketball. In our tiny world of the Parochial Athletic League (PAL), the school that has the best athletes that year generally excels at both flag football and basketball.

If selected to coach, I know the core seven or eight I will ask to play with us on the varsity comp team, but I need a few more. There is a new kid, a transfer, from another school in our league. I was told about him on shadow day. Shadow day is when new kids come to our school and shadow one of our students to get a feel for what a normal school day would be like. Invariably, the boys break off at recess and play a little pickup.

My son came home and told me about this kid from Cherryhill who might attend. He said the kid has game. I didn't get too excited. Thirteen-year-old boys have a tendency to overhype people, situations, and stories.

A transfer student is sort of like entering the NCAA transfer portal, in which a second-string quarterback loses his role to a better first stringer and realizes he will be better off starting at another school rather than waiting for an opportunity or an injury to the starter. But this, this is far less sinister. This is simply because some parents believe it is easier coming from our school because of its academic cachet to be admitted to the local private high school. Whether true or not, we get transfers all the time.

I never noticed Aaron at his other school last year because they had two eighth-grade basketball players who could ball. My first glimpse of him was in August on the football field. Within two passes I threw to the kid, I knew he can play hoops. Yes, I said hoops. At this level, it's just that easy to spot kids who can help you.

The final spot on our roster was and always has been our greatest enigma, Brian, the lone seventh grader I envisioned for the team. I had the privilege of coaching him when he was in fifth grade, and he played on our competitive JV team. I shouldn't really say I coached him, because he was hurt most of the season with a nagging calf injury. It was like the plot of the famous Beckett play *Waiting for Godot* in which two men famously wait for someone who never comes.

In our sixth-grade year, Brian played in our final game of the season and showed us a glimpse of what he could become. His father and I have a nice relationship. He really believes in his son, as do I. There was an overall jaundiced view of Brian's potential among our other families. They witnessed his fifth-grade season, always hearing he would soon be playing, only to be let down time and again. Our families are very much a "I'll believe it when I see it" group.

But I know differently. I know Brian has the "it" factor that no other child has had since I have been coaching at our small private school. There are very good athletes, don't get me wrong, but once in a blue moon there is someone with "it." The problem with "it" is that it is all potential until you do "it" with consistency in any and all settings and you quantify your "it" status. So much has to go right for a child with "it" to actually blossom into a full-fledged superstar. And it is too difficult to predict when that "it" will actually flourish into something. Parents, health, mental state of mind, desire, environment, opportunity—all factor into a child fulfilling their full potential.

Brian made former NBA player Matt Barnes's AAU team, played, and excelled with some of the finest talent in our area.

He has "it."

The real problem for his parents is that our league is not good enough for their son's talent. That seems pompous to say, but I truly believe that. There are times when playing with the best talent makes you better, and playing with equal, or less, talented kids actually drags your game down. I preach school pride to his father, but that only goes so far, as you can only imagine.

Their dilemma was to place their son in a public school known for its basketball or leave their son in this private school and prepare him for the education that they know will truly benefit him in the long run. This is a difficult equation to run in your mind when many people do not feel a middle school education amounts to much. But those people haven't been to our school. In my opinion, our middle school workload is more rigorous than the high school our boys will be attending. It was designed that way. Sounds ridiculous, but it's true.

SWEET JESUS!

We blew through the flag football season undefeated and only got scored upon once. The first playoff game was another blowout, and as we prepared for the biggest game of the year against our archrivals, St. Maximilian Kolbe, I was outside throwing the football with my sons when a text pinged my phone.

It read: *Can you talk?*

I respond, *Yes.*

It was the athletic director of our school.

Then my phone rang. I could hear his voice. It sounded sullen, downtrodden, sad. There was a pit in my stomach. The kind you get when you know bad news is coming.

"Good morning," he said.

"Good morning, Coach," I responded.

I call our AD "coach" because it is a moniker with a ton of respect behind it and he deserves that. If you have ever coached, it is what you want to hear. Rather than Mr. Whomever or your first name. It is meaningless to drop at will, but a man or woman who has truly dedicated their life to coaching, truly making children fundamentally better, truly helping a child find the joy in a sport, and giving of their time, has earned the moniker "coach." Our AD has earned it. Twenty-five years of teaching and summer basketball camps. How many children's lives impacted? How many smiles? How much joy?

Coach Swisher gets right to it: "You are the men's varsity comp coach at our school for this year."

Thank you, Jesus!

I am thrilled. I am thrilled to the point of tears.

He said there are two conditions: "You must be the only one on the bench. I want the boys to hear only one singular voice, yours. And, two, you must represent the school in a professional manner. There were times that you get a little ... errrr ... passionate. The headmaster wants you to be aware that you are representing our school."

"Dang," I said.

"I know you and I know the passion you bring. The headmaster just wants you to be aware."

My reputation preceded me. I knew that. To hear it from the head of our school was sobering. Reel in my antics. I was always respectful, just loud and aggressive. I needed to take this advice to heart if they were entrusting me with the program.

His decision was not without controversy though. The boys' home-room and social studies teacher, Coach Applewhite, who coaches the varsity comp team each year said he wanted the job too. The AD ruled in my favor.

"It is a unique situation," he had explained to Coach Applewhite. "Chris has been with these boys since kindergarten and his basketball style fits this team's personalities better."

Our core group of families is mostly behind this depending on the day they are asked. There are a few outliers whose sons will not make the team, whom I am certain will protest. Families whom I consider friends.

This is setting a bad a precedent for the school. Yup, this even happens in nonpaid coaching positions at small, private schools the world over.

Whatever the case, it is now my team … again.

My wife suggested I ask Coach Applewhite to help, to assist me. I know she is right. It is the right thing to do. I make the offer, but there is no response.

I know his answer.

I feel for him. The problem is I thought he would understand. I thought he would get it. He has two sons of his own, and I see how he is around them. A great dad. Why can't he see what this simply is—a father wanting to be with his son and the team who grew up together?

But then again, how can't I? This is what he loves too.

I have been assured by the school this has no bearing on his job. Of course, I would not want that. But I have some soul searching to do as well. Why do I want this so bad? Does this say something more about me?

Definitely.

See, I was okay when I was told I would not coach my oldest son, three years ago. Sure, I wanted to, but I did not have the same relation-ship with his friends that I do with these boys. As I mentioned, these boys were all in, together, not only at school, but at AAU tournaments that occupy entire weekends, where you truly see what you are made of. They all wanted to play together wherever and whenever we could. And most families were on the same page; most of these families were all in. If not, we hitched rides together, fed each other's kids, became parents to the entire group as needed.

It was different with my oldest son. And it is different with my youngest son too. Don't get me wrong, we all play school, recreation, and summer league ball together, but they don't all want to play AAU tournaments, the three games on a weekend at random and inconvenient times, disrupting, if not ruining a family's entire weekend. With my other sons, their friends' other sports come into play, which I know is totally healthy.

But not this team. This team was unique. Always has been. It's just different when you find eight families who buy into this same thing, even more unique when they are from the same school, even more special when the eight boys are from the same class of twelve boys. That is its uniqueness.

Eight families, a couple of dads, eight boys.

And this is our window. This is our chance to make history in our own small way.

The beauty in all this is that our AD recognizes this more than anyone. His first son just got married. His second son is in college. His youngest, a daughter, just went off to college. He and his wife are now empty nesters. He tells me it is quiet, like real quiet. He knows this is what I fear. We have talked about it. He remembers the life he had when his sons were young, how involved he was, and how much unprecedented fun he had. He remembers it.

Similarly, he has seen how involved I am with my sons; he has seen it firsthand at our school, in our community, at his summer camps. And maybe, in some small way, he wants to relive his time with his boys through me and these boys, those sacred times. He remembers. The moments. He gets it because he has already lived it and his personal window is now gone.

In many ways he and I are the same. He tells me. We share that bond. I know the dad he was (and is) and he sees my love not only for my own son, but for all of these boys. His nephew, Alex, happens to be one of them. He hears it from his brother and sister-in-law. He knows how his nephew feels about Coach Meyer and vice versa.

Alex lived through his seventh-grade year playing for Coach Applewhite. It was not a good year for him. He was relegated to the bench when, in my opinion, he was among the best players in the league as a seventh grader. His coach did these types of things to boys with less seniority, even if the younger boys were better players, or so it seemed.

In my opinion, the coach did not truly know the personalities of these boys. He did not truly study who they were, where they came from, and how they performed under stress, in battle. I have seen these boys in a variety of situations and games. You get to know who they are. What you can expect of them. How they react to different stressors.

In this particular instance, Alex could be seen as aloof to a casual observer, not really trying hard each day. In fact, this couldn't be further from the truth. He was one of the most competitive kids on the court. His way was to just coast, to glide. He was a glider. He would fight for the board or under the basket as aggressively as any, but he needed to be challenged, supported, and praised.

A good coach is as much a psychologist as a strategist.

This boy will be one of the best players in the league this year.

Look, I am blessed. I am blessed the school gave me an opportunity to coach my son. They didn't have to. And if I caused a controversy at our school, I am sorry. I truly am. I am lucky I have two other dads who will assist me and keep me in line, as they always do. I have a wife who has the perspective of ten sages. I have nine families who mostly want the same thing for their boys before we send them off to a high school so big, we all know our sons will be forced to be different than the protected children they can be for the next four more months we will spend together.

One thing is for sure: we all know the memories of these next four months will last a lifetime.

THE WEEK WAS not without further controversy. After being named the basketball coach, I was told I would be the only one allowed on the bench. Our AD said the rule came down from the headmaster. There was some jockeying for position, some calls to our AD, some emails—a way bigger distraction than it needed to be.

All coaches know you always need multiple coaches on the bench to see the floor more objectively, remind of playing time, say things to the boys in a different voice, help at practice. It is essential. So I knew I would have to talk with our headmaster. I have always found her to be fair and equitable with me. Although I am fairly certain she has more pressing issues at hand.

And I am not certain where this all started, but my worldview has always been quite simple.

Ultimately, we are all just dads.

I am not really a coach. It is not my vocation. It is not even my calling in some remote way. I do, however, have a ton of fun pretending. As I have said a million times over, I just want to be with my son and his friends.

That we have had some success makes it seem like I know what I am doing and enables me to immaturely tap into my youth for another small moment in time. The reality is, I do not know what I am doing. In fact, this is all the boys. Always has been. They just make me look like a coach because of their prowess and skill. You add my histrionics, screaming, and sideline antics, and, viola, they call me a coach.

I know I am not a coach. I am a dad having the time of his life. And all I've ever wanted is for all dads who want to join in on this journey to come aboard. Sit in the gym at practice, participate as they wish, experience on their own terms a nanosecond of memories we will all share. My mistake (and there have been many) is inclusion. I know how much I love being with these boys on their epic journey from childhood to manhood, and I don't want to be selfish. Come one, come all.

Now, however, in eighth grade, I find myself at the true precipice of childhood fun turning into big-time, local high school basketball. I hold absolutely no aspirations to go on from here, instead desiring to cling steadfastly to the fountain of youth that coaching provides me.

I still have my fourth grader Mack's epic team and what we are similarly building in a different but no less loving manner. I want to be with them and have fun. I seek the fun. I need the fun, for both me and the kids. Without the fun, this becomes a job. And I don't need another job.

But each passing year it gets tougher and tougher because the boys are all competing for fewer and fewer spots on the next grade's team. This is where youth athletics can get ugly. And I am part of it. No, I am a central figure in this ongoing and growing American tragedy.

My inclusion has been tested many times over the years by over-reaching parents. They always want more and are never seemingly satisfied with anything. At times it feels like the joy is literally being extracted from your veins like the blood sample you give the doctor.

What drives this? Why is it so important to make a team? These kids aren't scholarship material. They're not! What is this all for? To say your son made the team even if he is the fifteenth player on the squad? It makes no sense. It completely makes no sense.

At some point the parental white noise needs to be shut out and we need to close the doors and start building our team. At some point it needs to become just about us. That's my job. To provide the buffer between the overzealous parents and the team we are trying to build. This is no ordinary task. This will be our journey and we shall overcome. Together!

We won the flag football championship that fall for the first time in our school's history. Coach Quincy and I assisted Coach Roger. We beat our rivals in the semifinal game in the final seconds on a windy day. Aaron made a diving catch to get us close. Stevie found Alex in the corner of the end zone for a game-tying TD and then, with no time remaining, my son Brock slid and caught the extra point for the win. It was bedlam. After that dramatic win, the actual championship game victory was anticlimactic.

The news of all of us dads coaching was always hoped for, but now it was official. As I drove home from the championship game, I envisioned the basketball team that was only days away:

Brock, Tim, and Stevie would be my natural guards. Brock the shooter, Tim the driver, Stevie the point who can shoot. They are all very capable.

Dylan will play small forward or shooting guard. He and Brock have the most consistent shots on the team. But when Stevie is on, you keep feeding him.

Alex and Brian will man the boards and form an awesome forward center duo.

Aaron and Nick will come off the bench to provide front court depth, size, defense, and rebounding—and a few extra fouls. James will provide short bursts of nasty defense on an opposing team's best player. And Ben will provide guard and small forward depth.

Ten boys: nine eighth graders and a potential phenom of a seventh grader. It's time to get after it.

13

EARTH, WIND & FIRE AND
THE HIGHWAY PATROL

I was lucky in high school. As a junior, I played on an undefeated New York State small school (Class C) state championship football team. I was the third-string quarterback. I thought I was the second-string quarterback until the first-string quarterback got the flu before the state semifinal game and the coach placed another senior in the starting role ahead of me.

They didn't trust me.

I don't blame them.

I was a converted tight end with a rocket arm, but slow. Scotty O was the better choice. Our starting QB miraculously came back, and we won that game and the next one, too, to cap a perfect 10–0 season. Despite being third string, I played a ton. We were blowing out people regularly, and they wanted to see what they had for next year. I was second string in the blowouts, but third when it mattered.

The camaraderie of these guys was awesome. It was a special team and a great experience because the seniors were a close-knit, fun group of guys. They easily and graciously took me under their wing and made me feel like a part of the team. I was grateful for the experience.

I felt closer to that class than my own. That year, twenty-two seniors started at twenty-two total positions on the football field. I think everyone knew that next year was gonna be a rebuilding one.

I came out of that experience not wanting to put in what I knew was going to be a similarly intense amount of work to play basketball. I saw the heavily senior-laden lineup, and I was certain I did not want to ride the pines for yet another season. I made a radical choice by today's standards.

I chose not to play basketball.

I skipped my junior year because I was beaten down by football. My vision of running gassers on a team in which I might only, again, sparingly play proved all the motivation I needed.

In my mind, I could easily come back and play next year. I loved to play basketball, but the reality was I wanted to get a jump on the baseball season where I had a legitimate chance of starting. I had my baseball coach give me access to the middle school gym, and I set up the batting cage there in February. A friend and I were the first to start hitting and then, slowly, the other guys would trickle in as the weeks progressed. It paid off. I started at third the entire year. Playing regularly is way better than riding the pines, any day.

The basketball coach at our high school, Coach Caione, couldn't believe I didn't come out. He warned me that it was unheard of for someone to skip his junior year and then be relevant in his senior year. I looked him right in the eye. I could see he wanted me to play. But he was also a salesman. Even at this early age, I could see that. I was respectful and said thank you, but no thank you.

So I didn't play basketball my junior year of high school.

MY LOVE AFFAIR with Duke University started with my oldest brother's acceptance to the storied university in the fall of 1979. When he was admitted, I was a freshman in high school. The Duke stars of that four-year era were, among others, Gene Banks, Mike Gminski, Chip Engelland, and my brother's personal favorite, Mike Tissaw. (My brother later became a Greg Koubek disciple but Koubek never rose to the All-American status my brother swore he was destined to become.)

A high school friend of mine named Terry Singletary was nicknamed Duke at our high school because his sister had gone to Duke as well. She later became a local newscaster in the Raleigh-Durham area. Terry was a heavyset African American kid with a smile and personality as large as his belly. He was the most popular kid not only in our school, but the entire town. Everybody loved Duke.

I distinctly remember the road trip we took when my middle brother was a senior, Terry was a junior, and I was a sophomore in 1981, which was, ironically, Coach Krzyzewski's first year at Duke.

One February break, for reasons still unknown to me to this very day, our parents let us drive to Durham, North Carolina, from our silver-spooned, insulated hamlet of Pleasantville, New York, in Terry's parents' poop brown Lincoln Continental Town Car. Yup, the massive, boat-like car you would imagine seeing in a *Shaft* movie equipped with an eight-track player. Now, my parents never played Earth, Wind & Fire at home, but soon enough their porcelain-ed, green-eyed, baby boy knew every word to "Shining Star," "Let's Groove," and "Boogie Wonderland."

To this day, it was the most epic road trip I have ever been on. We stopped for fast food everywhere, burped and farted the whole way, ate Slim Jims and junk food, and only got stopped once by the police, somewhere south of Richmond, when a white police officer stuck his face in the driver's side window and saw the three of us:

"How— What— How old are you?"

"Fifteen, sixteen, and seventeen, sir."

"Where are your … your plates say New York."

"Yes, sir. Pleasantville to be exact," I said with my voice cracking.

More stares.

A really awkward beat.

"Can I ask, what the hell is going on here?"

"We are going to see our brother at Duke University, sir."

Now the cop retracts as he looks at the color of Terry's skin.

"Their brother, my sister," Terry clarified.

Even more confusion.

"They're not the same person. They're ... they both live down there."

"And your parents let you drive a Lincoln Town Car, from New York, along southern highways, to do that?"

"Isn't that awesome?" Terry smiled widely.

The cop just shook his head and pulled his head out of the driver's side window: "Slow down!"

He marched back to his car.

"I think I just crapped myself," my brother said.

"Shhhh."

Now sticking his hands down the back of his pants, he said, "Nope, I know I just crapped myself."

"He's letting us go."

"Does anyone have toilet paper?"

"No way," Terry whispered looking closely in the rearview mirror. "He's leaving. Guys? He's leaving!"

And off sped the police car.

We turned to each other for a beat and then burst out laughing.

I am thankful the Child Protective Services statute of limitations has run out on that one.

My brother had told me how insane the basketball games were at Cameron Indoor Stadium. Terry and I wanted to see for ourselves. We had never seen a stadium where big-time college basketball was played. So we gathered some IDs from my brother's fraternity brothers and headed over.

We walked out of my brother's frat house and saw a college campus like you see in the movies: dorms on either side of a grassy quad, kids hanging out, playing Frisbee, and chatting. A gorgeous baroque cathedral standing majestically, in reverence, at the end of a long quad as if to remind the students to behave.

The campus is sick. One of the most beautiful in America, or so I am told. I do remember looking around this picturesque campus as I slowly walked, thinking, crap, my brother really gets to go here?

We walked over to Cameron Indoor Stadium. A kid watching the entrance saw us in our shorts and told us we couldn't play there. We asked if we could just take a look. He asked to see our IDs. Terry and I flashed the IDs my brother's frat brothers had given us. The guy at the door looked at them, then up at us.

He handed them back with a smile.

Just for a minute.

We then realized Terry's ID was of a white guy.

Terry and I stepped in and looked at this majestic, shrine-like stadium. It was as if we heard a choir of hoop angels singing from the rafters. Even at this time, I swear you could feel how special it was. For me, this is where ACC basketball was played. This is where Gene Banks fed Mike Gminski for his jump hook. This is where the Tar Heels' Jimmy Black and Mike O'Koren, a kid from Cardinal Hayes in the Bronx, and a Jersey boy, took it to the Blue Devils.

This was no ordinary basketball gym. No, this is where the games I watched on my TV on Saturdays were actually played. And this is where the greatest coach in college basketball of my time was about to build the greatest college program of my time for some forty years at the same university.

I was there when it all started. Just unreal in retrospect.

Terry and I paid our respects and found the rec gym where we could actually play some pickup.

Terry looked older than a high school senior, so he rolled in and immediately called next game. I loved watching his self-assured bravado.

As we laced up, we looked at each other and just smiled. We couldn't believe we were here, at Duke, about to play in a college pickup game as high schoolers. And me, the guy who didn't even play basketball this year, had no idea what to expect. These were college kids.

"Just do your thing," Terry said, as I nodded nervously.

And it started.

You just start running, watch the flow of the game, try not to stand out, and go set some picks. And within the second time down the court, Terry got it on the wing and just ripped it. I started smiling because, like the drunk at your local bar, Terry never turned down a shot and often had to be reined in by our coaches. That dude would rip it from anywhere. I loved that about him. Like the honey badger, homie didn't care. And I knew that. And I also knew where the ball was going because Terry missed a ton. So I'd position myself under the hoop for the rebound and easy putback or kick right back out to him where he would immediately just rip it again. The honey badger didn't care.

And it happened just like that.

People start passing and picking and rolling and driving. It's like poetry in motion, a Bolshoi ballet really. The movements of the ball are elegant and beautiful to watch and witness and study. But I knew I was one of the youngest out there, so I held no grand illusions of scoring. I just wanted to fit in and get a good sweat.

And we did.

And Terry could sweat. Dude was a legit sweater. Like a gland issue.

And after a few games, we headed back to my brother's frat house. On our walk back, we dried off and talked.

"Dude, you can play," Terry said to me.

"Whattaya mean?"

"You can play. Why didn't you play this year?"

"I couldn't sit anymore."

"Nah, you wouldn't sit. You can flat out play."

I smiled.

Terry was always kind, but he meant what he said. He wouldn't bullshit you and I appreciated that. Just hearing those words from him gave me confidence. You talk about a good dude. Everybody loved Duke.

We drank beers on Wednesday night with my brother and his college friends, waking up and playing basketball if not at, but near, Cameron, sneaking into the lunchroom for food, and watching coeds walk to class in this exquisite college setting.

Pure magic!

That I got to do it two years in a row, a true gift.

Duke, the person and the place, are basketball magic to me.

14

HOW WE ROLL

To say I was looking forward to coaching again was a colossal under-statement. Sure, I had been coaching my youngest son's team in my year away, but I missed these boys. I don't think I missed coaching them as much as I missed being with them in the grind. The grind is the daily, weekly, monthly time we all put in together to create something special. The practices are long (an hour and a half), three days a week plus games. It becomes long hours.

But that's the fun. The times we get to just be with one another in our happy place. The security of the gymnasium. Our sanctuary away from all the outside world requires of us.

In some strange way I found peace here.

But not without some early drama.

As we started our first practice, Brian, our seventh grader, the kid who has "it," the kid whom I believe will be the best basketball player of all of them, and who played one game for us in fifth grade, was not here. He has pneumonia. His father told me the doctor has said he is out for the first month.

It is the kiss of death. This will kill morale, and I immediately suspect he will not be with us this season. My other two coaches say forget about him and move on. I hold out hope, not only because his father and I are friends, but selfishly because I know he will take us to another level.

He has "it."

EVERY PRACTICE LOOKED eerily similar, except for the nuances we installed for the team we were playing that upcoming week.

The practices went like this:

Lay-ups and jumpers (10 minutes): technique, proper foot jump off, use glass
 Right
 Left
 Center
 Obstructed (being hit with a pool noodle)

Dribbling and fast break drills (5 minutes)
 Crab drill, how to approach rim from the wings on fast break
  w/o ball
 Heavy ball
 Oversized ball
 Regular ball

Defense (15 minutes)
 Man vs. Zone vs. 4-1 "man-zone"
 Technique, right hand, belly button, force left
 Rotation in man and zone; How to use out of bounds as a defender

Boxing out, find man, use your butt
Outlet and fill lane
Upcoming team

Water break (5 minutes)

The press and press break (10 minutes)
KD
UNO
Butter

Inbounds and side-out plays (10 minutes)
Stack
Cross
Tick
Quad

Offense (15 minutes)
vs. man-to-man
vs. zone
Pick-and-roll
The bounce pass
Back door

Run lines (10 minutes), full out, no pacing yourselves

Foul shooting (10 minutes), must be done when trying to simulate game situations

WASH YOUR HANDS, PUT A HAT ON, GO DO YOUR HOMEWORK!

GET OUTTA OUR KITCHEN

Here's the thing. No one likes to practice. No one! All the boys want to do is scrimmage. Play games and scrimmage in practice. It's easy and most coaches let this happen.

I am not a fan of scrimmaging in practice.

I am a fan of repetition. Extreme repetition and fundamentals. Repeating fundamentals over and over again. Ya dig? And I think children respond to that. They know what to expect and they come to know what is expected of them. So it is mostly the same thing every practice.

I am also a huge fan of defense, or D. I like defense more than I like offense. I have found that most kids do not like defense because, to play it well, it takes a lot of work. It is difficult. It takes heart. It takes grit. It is dirty. And there are, generally, not the overt cheers from the crowd when you shut someone down as there are when you put the ball in the basket.

And we all like the cheers.

Most onlookers cheer only when a basket goes in. I cheer when I see something nasty on D.

D rules my world.

In our little gym, we talk about not letting anyone into our kitchen. You don't want someone coming into your kitchen to steal your food. The rim and its close proximity are our kitchen. The opposition scoring is stealing our food. We need to prevent opponents from stealing our food. I want them to preserve the rim, prevent buckets, and, most importantly, hold sacred our space around the rim, our kitchen. When that happens, good things ripple out from there: we prevent buckets, rebound, start the fast break, and we bum-rush their kitchen. That's how we roll.

Keep outta our kitchen!

The other most salient point about defense in my eyes is that it is never truly about your man beating you. This is a strange sounding concept to most because we think of one defender covering "his" guy, on the court five guys on five guys. But I don't think like that.

See, at this age, we all get beat. Like in life, we all get beat. If we didn't, the ball would never move up the court. Everyone gets beat. So, with this in mind, we talk about four fundamental ideals:

1. PRESSURE:

Keep pressure on your man full court. Get up on him, swipe at the ball, get your hands on him, run with him. If you do this for four quarters, you are gonna tire out most kids. You tire them out and their jump shots start coming up a few inches short in the fourth quarter because their legs are tired. (All shots come from a player's legs.) Missed shots in the fourth quarter are good for our team.

The analogy I always use is this: It's like being a good boxer. A good boxer doesn't just hit his opponent as hard as he can as fast as he can. That's not boxing. A good boxer works the other guy's body, not because his opponent is guarding his face with his gloves, but because if he works the body repeatedly, round after round, his opponent will get tired and, slowly, over time, start to drop his hands. When he drops his hands because he is getting tired from all the body shots, his head becomes exposed. When an opponent's head is exposed, a knockout may be imminent.

Another important fundamental we talk about is this one:

2. HELP D:

How your other four brothers behind you react to the first man getting beat in front of them. We are all playing man-to-man defense. Man-to-man with one eye on the ball. We call it a "man-zone." When, or if, the ball defender on our team gets beat, the nearest guy, or two, must rotate to the ball and shut down the dribbler's access to the rim.

When we properly rotate off our man, we are thus leaving our man undefended behind us, which means another one of my team-mates must then rotate to my man, especially near the rim. If we are constantly rotating to the man who is open nearest to the rim, then good things will happen. In a worst-case scenario, one of our brothers won't be able to rotate to the open man who is far enough away from the rim. We would rather be slow or unable to rotate to an offensive man farther away from the rim for a jump shot, than a man under the rim for a lay-up.

In this rationale, we are simply playing the percentages, figuring a lay-up is what we want to defend first because it is a higher percentage shot than a jumper or three pointer farther away from the basket. (A lay-up is generally a 90% successful shot vs. a three pointer with its 40% success rate for NBA-level three-point shooters, and we are not playing NBA-caliber three-point shooters.)

It's all math at the end of the day.

In order to do this effectively, I come to my third major point:

3. CONDITIONING:

No one likes to run and get into playing shape. In basketball gyms since the beginning of time, you run lines, gassers, suicides, whatever a coach might call them. They are always the same thing. Everyone starts out spread across one of the baselines. When the coach blows the whistle, everyone races to the foul line and touches the floor, then sprints back to the same baseline they just left.

Without stopping, they touch that baseline and then sprint back to now the midcourt line. They touch that and sprint back to the baseline. There are four major lines on the floor: foul line, half court line, other foul line, other baseline. When everyone touches all four lines and gets back to the original baseline, that is running one line/gasser/suicide.

It is key to make the boys touch each line with their hand because that involves them bending down. They all try to cheat two ways: They don't bend all the way down to touch the line, and they don't sprint the entire way. Someone always cheats and someone always dogs it. Why?

Because they don't know how many lines you are gonna make them run so they are trying to preserve their energy. And they get good at disguising how hard they are running. Some just coast, some make stressed facial movements, some flail their arms, others look me in the eye as if to say stop, you sadomasochist.

And some kids can't run at all. Don't mind that, just keep them running at their pace and make them finish with the other ones clapping encouragement. This is good team building for everyone, the fast guys as well as those slower. And we are a team no matter what.

The number of lines we run is commensurate with how well the team did in practice or the previous games. Poor plays and mistakes, more gassers; good games and practices, fewer lines. But they gotta run. Their conditioning will pay off at the end of the games when things are close. I have seen it. If your boys never get tired, you will win more games than you will lose, guaranteed. The number of cheap baskets you will get in a game because of your conditioning (hustle) is a ton. If you truly study the game, you will see.

The last ideal we speak of is this one:

4. I NEED EVERY LOOSE BALL:

If you can't get on the ground and win every loose ball, tell yo momma to pack you a blankie because you will need it to keep yourself warm next to me, on the bench! I simply can't have people on the court who won't dive for everything. This is difficult to understand because the basketball floor is called hardwood for a reason. It's hard. And when you dive on it, you get floor burns, bruises, and bumps; it hurts. But if you get five like-minded guys doing this for every loose ball, good things will happen.

You stress these four fundamental ideals and you will have a good year.

THE FOUR

While there is always the chance that one of the schools has a 6 foot 4 transfer student from Lithuania enroll at their school in the fall, there are three teams that should fight for championship contention along with us: Northern California Prep School, St. Maximilian Kolbe (SMK), and St. Bede the Venerable (SBV).

Northern California Prep School is the team that beat us when we were 17–1 in sixth grade. Five to six kids on their squad can really play, and they are well coached by a former star player from the CBA and European Leagues, Dave Ancrum. It is the most expensive middle school in our region, and former Sacramento Kings great Peja Stojakovic's children went there, among others.

I swear they recruit basketball players—kids who could clearly not afford it but who are there on what I believe are basketball scholarships. I did not think this was possible, but I believe this to be true. A few years back they had one of the best eighth graders ... in America! He dunked on us—yes, in eighth grade. That is not supposed to happen in eighth-grade parochial basketball in our area. I saw it with my own eyes. And he had two teammates that year that I thought were even better than he was. Something is not right over there.

Only a little sour grapes.

St. Maximilian Kolbe (SMK) is our local rival down the street. Many kids play with us on various AAU teams and other local rec teams, and their parents are friends whom we all like and see around town—until game time. They always play us close and the two teams know each other like the backs of our hands. No real surprises here.

This year, they match up well with us and they never give up. They were also well-coached formerly by another dad who has been going toe-to-toe with me since these boys were in first grade in our local rec league (a great father who, like me, simply enjoys being with his son) and now by one of the freshman basketball coaches for the high school team most of the boys will be attending. Another great guy. While we compete and want to pound each other into the ground on the court, we can smile and shake hands, if not hug, afterward.

St. Bede the Venerable (SBV) has the best player in the league, aside from the boys on my team. Correction, not the best player, just the most aggressive. This child has always been among the best players in our league. He, too, has grown up with us locally. He excels at every sport: baseball, soccer, flag football, and hoops—the best player in all the leagues.

A tenacious rebounder, fast, and nasty. He is a great kid but never had a complete team around him. As such, he is not a team player and tends to want to do everything himself. These kids are the easiest to defend. Send four guys at him every time, and he will never give up the rock. Even when he scores twenty, you win by twenty. He needs to be coached properly.

The truth of the matter is that any of these teams, and a few others, could beat any one of us on any given night if the boys were up too late playing NBA 2K, Madden, or Fortnite, had a cold, were mad at their parents, or just not themselves.

Anything can happen at this age—and has.

THE ENDANGERED SPECIES: ZEBRAS

The refs suck.

This is every boy's complaint when things don't go as he planned. When they are being tested. When they are struggling. When they know in their gut they are not achieving like they should be. By now they recognize their own poor play, they know it, they see it within themselves.

Rather than simply closing their mouths and trying harder, fourteen-year-olds often cast out at the most likely and vulnerable culprit, just like it is when they blame their younger sibling for everything. The refs' black and white stripes form an incandescent bull's-eye in these boys' minds.

I, however, do not share their enthusiasm.

In our local area, a business handles the placement of all the referees for the local middle school, high school, and AAU gyms.

There is a massive shortage of referees. Wonder why?

A bunch of kids and their *Glory Days* coaches thinking they can do no wrong because everything they do on the court is immaculate and pristine hardwood perfection.

In most instances, the refs are paid fifty bucks and asked to drive all over the county to gyms where they are abused by crowds, coaches, and sometimes players. We do not benefit by instant replay, and many of these local games are filled with the intensity of championship games, due to school, town, or league rivalries. I would venture a guess that these men and women are never complimented on how well they refereed a game—even when they have done an excellent job.

What type of person wants to do that?

With this in mind, I tell my players to never let the refs decide the outcome of a game. Do your job, and only your job, and the referees shouldn't come into play. Assume you will never get a foul call, and all calls will go against you. That is how well you have to play. If you set your expectation at zero, you will never be let down.

As a coach, you have to understand this. But you also have to work the refs. You have to know the appropriate way to ask them a question in a manner, and at a time, that will not embarrass them, and you will get their attention, and perhaps a few calls, if done properly.

When you chastise them out loud, you will not get the calls. I have found this out firsthand. I have been "T-d" up (AAU only). I have been thrown out of gyms (again AAU and only happened once and I was protecting my kids from getting hurt, in my mind), and I have learned doing it in a calm, unobtrusive manner is always the best. In our league, it has been requested of us to simply raise a hand and ask to speak to the ref during a time-out or quarter break. They will acknowledge you if you get their attention in this manner. To my surprise, it has worked.

I cannot imagine that this would work at most AAU tournaments.

The refs are human beings who do this to make a little extra money in a sport or sports they most likely enjoy. They deserve our respect, even if they blow a few calls a game.

No one, let alone me, is perfect.

Everyone, please teach your children this.

15

THE COBBLER AND
ME, A LOVE STORY

After not playing my junior year, my senior season looked strong. We had two brothers from the legendary first family of basketball in our town—Brad and his younger brother, David—one kid from the Abbott House, Floyd James, and finally Dr. J's co-player of the year, Jim Bergholtz, as our coach. All of my childhood influences had now converged onto one team.

We started out the year by playing in a larger school's holiday tournament, and I guarded, man-up, a seven-footer named Ewing (not Patrick) from Somers High School. I scored twenty-nine the first night and then came back with fifteen in the championship game taking down the host school, Kennedy High, in a massive upset.

Our fans stormed the court.

All of my teammates thought I was going to be named Most Valuable Player of the tournament because we won it all. I sat there grinning as the all-tournament team was announced. When I wasn't on that list, my teammates started chanting: "MVP! MVP! MVP!"

When the PA announced the tournament's Most Valuable Player, it was Dan Kovaleski, a player from the host school's team, who went for twenty-five in both games, despite their loss.

I was crushed. My teammates patted me on the back and said I was robbed. People came out of the stands and told me the same.

Maybe my coach, who presciently gave me that warning a year prior when I decided to skip my junior year, was right; there was no way to skip a year and still be relevant.

It stung for a few hours, but my teammates and my coach made me feel better. And I continued playing well. By midyear I was among the leading scorers and rebounders in our league. The local paper wrote an article about me saying something like, Where did this kid come from? Coach Caione (the man who would've coached me in my junior year) was interviewed for the article. He told them I would be an all-county performer if he was still coaching and that I got robbed at the Kennedy tournament.

Reading his quote was all the vindication I needed.

Somehow this tiny paper, this *Patent Trader* newspaper with a circulation of maybe two hundred, written by a local sports reporter named Wayne Barrett, complete with not one, but two, action photos of me, and my almost coach's words in print made it all ... better?

We played my senior year and finished 18–5. We lost to the same team in our league three separate times; one of their kids, a 6 foot 7 shooting guard named Brian Fitzpatrick, went on to play Division 1 at Yale and another, a 6 foot 10 stork of a man named Jeff Dumas, went on to play at "The" Ohio State University in Columbus. Big Ten hoops.

It was demoralizing to lose to the same team in our division three times, but they were simply better than we were, and I had the time of my life playing with my friends and Coach Bergholtz, whom I adored.

But, oddly enough, what I remember most about that year was a small boy who was a junior on our team. He was probably the twelfth man on our team of twelve and played one sport and one sport only, basketball.

Kenny Cartisano was an undersized, slow, stout, lefty guard with a pretty decent shot. And before every one of our practices, he would challenge me to a little one-on-one, just for fun. And we did have fun together. We were not close friends away from the basketball court. We didn't hang out at each other's homes. But here, in the safety and sanctity of our practice gym, with the shared love of our sport, we were teammates.

I loved his smartass quips when he drained one in my face and how he challenged me even when I was clearly bigger, stronger, and better. I admired him more than he knows because he came out for the team. He showed up and pounded. He put the same amount of time in as everyone, and he worked his ass off. It hurt him. You could see it was a struggle at times. He was shorter, rounder, and had not just played an entire football season running around in the heat and practicing six days a week, like many of us.

Respect.

I remembered that he hadn't scored all season, and we were blowing out a team, so he got a chance to play. When he went in, the entire bench was locked arm-in-arm, even more excited than when we were in the game ourselves. Each time down the court, we were cheering for Kenny to get a bucket.

Then, there he was, sitting in the corner (his favorite spot), a place where he felt comfortable. A place where he had drained it in my very face many times as I leaped to block his shot with my outstretched five fingers, trying to obstruct his view of the basket.

And then, just like that, one of our guards fed him. He was right in front of our bench in the right corner. He caught it, never even hesitated for a second, and let it fly.

It was as if time went into slow motion.

The entire bench rose to their feet in unison.

The shot sailed in the air for what seemed like an eternity before swooshing perfectly through the net.

Our bench, the entire student body cheering section behind us, and the entire crowd-filled gymnasium broke out in uncontrolled pandemonium as he high-fived us grinning from ear to ear and hustled back down the court to play defense.

The gym literally erupted as if we had won the biggest game of our high school's history in dramatic fashion at the buzzer. Everyone in that gym knew about Kenny's first bucket.

Amid all the hysteria around us, I remember looking up at the head of the bench and meeting eyes with Coach Bergholtz. We both just smiled.

Coach knew right then, right at that moment, this team was different, that we were special. If we had that kind of bond with each other, we were gonna be a force.

But, to be completely honest, my true fondness for Kenny derived from his father, Mr. Cartisano. He was a cobbler in the neighboring town for my entire seventeen years of life up to that point. My mother would go to him for all her shoe needs. He was a craftsman, like a legit artist. He would make shoes look like brand new again. He was gifted in a time when shoes were made well and cobblers mattered. A great time.

At first glance, it seemed like Mr. Cartisano had a little chip on his shoulder. In fact, as a child growing up, I don't believe I ever saw the man smile. I was generally scared to walk into his store, kinda like approaching Grendel's secret lair somewhere deep in an Old English marsh. In reality, I am fairly certain his demeanor was brought on by the demanding customers of Chappaqua, the tony hamlet where the Clintons, hedge fund CEOs, and the like, among others, now reside. He wasn't particularly friendly, and I would run in and pay for my mom and dad's shoes now and again throughout my childhood.

Then, I had a serious problem.

My baseball glove had a tear in it. Back in the mid-seventies, you had one baseball glove for your entire life. Mom and Dad either bought you a real large one and you made the best of it, or, more likely, it was a hand-me-down from your older brother. My oldest brother was an amazing baseball player who taught me all about the proper care for your things like cleats (we used to shine them with that white, liquid stick, if you remember?) and baseball mitts. I learned it all from my older brother, something for which he never gets his due credit.

Well, my brother taught me that caring for your glove would yield dividends in return. Almost like some zen shit, if you put good karma out into the world, it would return tenfold. This was something he had learned at one of the baseball camps he attended. We would Vaseline the leather glove (yes, petroleum jelly), place a ball in the pocket, and wrap it tightly with five or six rubber bands.

Well, my glove was softer than a baby's arse. That glove was literally an extension of my left hand to me; no, better than my left hand because it made some sick catches I couldn't have done without it. I had taken such good care of it (just like my brother told me) and it had made me the player I was at a young age. And I could field. I literally thought that glove was part of me.

Then, I got a tear in it.

I got a tear in my glove from using it so much. It was tragic, like really tragic. I thought if this tear in the pocket of my glove kept going, the glove would be rendered useless and I would have to break in a new one. Even at this young age, I knew a new glove would take years to break in, no matter how much I Vaselined it. The dirt, the hand oils, the heat and sun that made a glove a glove took years of "professional" use to make it the way I had my old glove. And like Thor with his hammer, or Rapunzel with her hair, I needed that damn glove to play baseball.

So my mom suggested I bring my glove to Mr. Cartisano. I said, "The creepy guy you bring your shoes to?"

She smiled and nodded.

I asked her if she would take it in for me because I am only ten years old. And to her credit, she insisted I go in, explain my problem, and see if maybe he can help.

Thanks a frickin' lot, Mom.

But it was worth a shot. This is my glove. My compatriot in a game I love. It was part of me.

As a young child, I am not gonna lie when I tell you, I had some anxiety about this. He wasn't exactly Captain Happy winning congeniality awards at the local Kiwanis Club, and now I had to take my baby in there to see if he could help. A shoe guy.

So I worked up enough courage to finally do it. I had games coming up and the tear was getting worse with each practice. I could see that. There could be no more putting this off. It must go down now. I had to do this!

My mom pulled up to the front of his store and saw me just staring at its entrance for a long beat. She finally said, "Go on!"

I shuffled in and took a deep breath. I did not see Grendel at the cash register. But there was clearly an open, non–glass-filled window cut into the sheetrock showing the back room of his shop, the room where Mr. Cartisano worked on the shoes. Then, his head slowly peered out at me at the front of the store, looking directly at me over the glasses perched on the edge of his nose. We made eye contact. No words.

I put my head down and sped up toward the register.

He came out, spoke no words, and I, immediately and nervously, spewed out my predicament. He listened attentively and reached for my baby. I handed it over. He studied it. Then, he put his hand inside of it—without asking! Now it's getting personal. He slapped his fist in the pocket and turned it over to inspect the back side. He really studied that glove, but now I could see his respect. His memories of playing, his reverence.

Then he said, "I don't think I can do anything here. I'm a cobbler. I just work on shoes."

He opened the glove up, shaking his head.

"See this tear? Whatever I do will just keep ripping, it'll never be the same."

All the wind came out of me. I was crestfallen.

His eyes immediately shot over the glove to mine. He noticed the sadness on my face.

"Okay, thank you." I grabbed my glove, turned, and walked away.

As I reached for the door, I heard, "You're the Meyer boy, right?"

"Yes, sir," I barely mumbled in a downtrodden voice.

"Lemme see what I can do."

My eyes perked up. I turned and I was beaming. I ran my glove back to him—

"Thank you. Thank you, Mr. Cartisano."

And Mr. Cartisano, the cobbler, the guy who only works on shoes, repaired my baseball glove. It was better than I could have ever dreamed of. He made all kinds of apologetic excuses about how his repair job might not hold because of this or that. I didn't even hear one of them. He made that thing look better than before.

Heck, with that new piece of leather machine-stitched into the webbing of my old glove, it felt, in some strange way, like brand new again. Like it had new life. And now it had this badge. This badge of honor, this repair that said, I used this thing so damn much that I tore a hole in the pocket and then had it fixed to wreak even more havoc on the baseball diamond.

I was in heaven. Literally in heaven, and he could see it.

I handed him the twenty-dollar bill my mom told me to give him, but he said, "No charge."

I looked up at him with a furrowed brow. "No charge?"

He saw I didn't understand. "Go make a great catch."

So now, all these many years later, his son Kenny and I played on our varsity high school basketball team together having that dream season.

After the season had just ended, Mr. Cartisano came up to me and we were talking about our magical year and our trip to play in the County Center, the Madison Square Garden of Westchester County.

He was beaming from ear to ear telling me how well we did, how amazing we were, how fun it was for him to be at every single one of our games, home or away, it didn't matter, he was there—and Kenny didn't play that much. But you could see there was a genuine joy on this man's face. You could see how much he truly enjoyed that one season of all our lives sitting on those rock-hard gym bleachers cheering on his son's high school basketball team.

And he went on and on, never really even making eye contact with me as people often do when they are lost in the moment of describing happy things they remember. He even had me smiling from ear to ear just watching him as he itemized all the great things we did as a team. He knew every minute detail of our victories and our losses. He was a student of the game, he really watched those games and had great insights. It was impressive.

Then, he abruptly stopped and the joy seemed to vanish from his face.

There was a real awkward silence as I watched him look down at his shoes and search, no, struggle, for his next words.

His head then slowly raised and he looked directly at me. Tears now filled his eyes.

"You know what was the best part?"

I shook my head.

"How nice you were to Kenny through it all."

I smiled awkwardly not really knowing what he meant.

"Kenny told me every day about your one-on-ones before practice. He told me about every one of them. And then I saw how you all jumped for joy when he scored at the end of the Mahopac game."

I started to smile and nod. I remembered those moments too.

A long beat.

"Do you know how much joy you brought to my son's life?"

I shook my head.

"And do you know how much joy that brought me?"

We were locked on each other's eyes.

"You're a good kid. Your parents raised you right."

And he turned and walked away.

And I just watched him walk off down the hall.

I'm not sure I ever saw Mr. Cartisano again after that day.

For some reason, that moment in time, that short conversation we shared, was way better than any of the eighteen games we won that year.

I remember that day like it was yesterday.

16

SHIT SANDWICH

We were set to scrimmage a local school, St. Mary's School of the Sacred Heart (SMSSH), in our first action of the year. We knew them well. We were the better team. As coaches, we talked about not showing them too much of our offense, defense, or full-tilt press. We planned to go into the scrimmage with the idea of simply running against some real competition. We wouldn't play our normal rotation, but instead would let everyone get plenty of PT, and move on.

I hate these games.

The reality is we were supposed to play in a tournament, but it was canceled. I would have much preferred to see where we stood, at this juncture, when there was a tournament win at stake. It's just different.

But our players were ready to play a team other than themselves in a game-like scenario. There is some trepidation in the air because no one knows who will start or how long they will play. I created two groups of teams. We didn't start the best five. The scrimmage would last five quarters so there should be plenty of playing time for everyone.

In the first half, our play was lackluster. The boys were even or getting handled most of the half. I don't know what it is, but there are times as a coach when you just sit back and watch, when you try not to comment on every little thing, and you see the opposing team get every loose ball, make a series of crazy shots, and lull your team into complacency and a lack of hustle.

The overall feeling is the other team simply wants it more. You try, for a moment, to be an objective observer and witness this aside and apart from being the coach, to just let it be, to just let them play.

But I can't stand that.

Now to be fair, our goal was not to show the opposition too much, to run our offense, not press, and to get our legs back in this first competition of the year. In doing so, we really didn't look that good. And as it was our first competition against another team, you try not to get too worked up about the performance. After all, it's our first time-out there this year.

Why do I have such a difficult time doing this?

Then their coach, a great father and local real estate agent in our community, walked over during the game and whispered to me, "Where's the press?"

"Huh?"

"The press, the press, that killer press of yours?" he said, almost annoyed.

"I wasn't gonna press today, Coach," I responded.

"Why not?"

"I didn't want to show you anything."

He laughed. But I could see it's the laugh of "come on, dude." So I said, "Would you like me to?"

"Well yeah, that's what you're known for. I wanna see how my boys react."

"You got it. Which one you wanna see?"

Now he looked me in the eye and paused for a beat. I saw fear. Like deer-in-the-headlights fear. He thought we just had one press. He doesn't know we have four. He doesn't know these boys have been pressing since third grade. I could see by the way he looked at me that he was now concerned. He is a dad like me. Like me, he probably just wanted to coach his son to be with him one last year before he goes off to high school. He didn't suspect the "which press do you want to see" comment.

He turned away and said, "Any one is fine."

And we do. We didn't want to, but we do. It's a scrimmage for both teams and we wanted to provide the opportunity for them to get better just as they are providing us that same opportunity. We are not that cutthroat. We are friends in the community with one another and all our families interact and see each other at the grocery store, pizza joint, or sports fields. There is a common bond. As competitive as we are, we will all be friends with one another as our children grow. Our community transcends sports.

So we pressed. It looked awkward, and quite bad at times, but we pressed. They broke it quite easily the first two times, and you could visibly see our players breaking down for fear of it not working. The confidence on their faces was becoming unglued, unhinged actually, in the short span of two times down the court.

As the coach, I saw this and tried to patch the leaks in our press on the fly: move a guy back on that side, up on the other, move the middle guy in front, instead of aside their player. Every press needs that constantly. No press works perfectly or exactly as you practice it.

And then it happened.

One of our players in his complete fourteen-year-old-ness changed the press on his own, and the others listened to him. I noticed it happening and yelled, "We are in a 1 x 3 x 1 zone press," and he yelled back, "It was not working, so we changed it."

TIME-OUT!

I stopped the scrimmage on the spot.

GET OFF THE COURT!

I pulled the entire team off the court and replaced them with the five guys on the bench. I said nothing and told the refs we were ready to go.

The team just sat there pissed they had been yanked in the middle of the game but knowing exactly why.

If I didn't correct that insurrection in this first game experience of the year, I would have lawlessness throughout the year, and I would not be able to coach. These boys needed to relearn some respect. And whether it was because of the comfort they have with me and Coach Quincy or simply the way the fourteen-year-old mind works, this had to be stopped instantly, or I would lose the team. You lose the team and it's gonna be a long year.

When the half ended, I had all the boys sit. I looked a few right in the eye without calling out names. There is an intimacy in a basketball huddle that is lost on no one. The close proximity of everyone and the looking in each other's eyes is all you need to know, hear, and see. The boys all know who I am talking to and when they need to take owner-ship or respond. There is nothing held back in our huddle.

I explained I simply could not have them changing the plays in the middle of the game. Under no circumstance do I want that to ever hap-pen again. I explained the need for constant tweaks and adjustments to the press and how this must happen on the fly, but never change what we are in.

They get it. No apologies, but they get it.

I then went further. I know they needed this. I wanted to em-power them.

"This does not mean you are never to speak. I want your opinion, if you see something, if you feel something is not working, I want to know about it. I want to hear about it. I value what you have to say because you are playing, I am not."

They get it. They know what they did was wrong. I don't ask who initiated it because I don't care. They got the message.

We went back out there and turned a five-point deficit into a twenty-four point victory. Our press will do that to people.

With our first scrimmage now in the books, I returned home to an email from the head of our league. It said the league had officially instituted the "all play" rule at all levels of league play, including our own, the varsity comp division, the seventh and eighth grades' most competitive division.

With this new rule, the league is now *mandating* all team players must play 25% of the game, or one full quarter. *Must!* Each game will be stopped by the referees halfway through each quarter (at the 3:30 mark) for substitutions to happen. The home team will be responsible for the scorebook. The visiting team will be responsible for making certain all players play the mandatory 25% of the game. If a player is pulled at any time in his three minute and thirty second half of a quarter, no portion of his time played will count as his time played. He *MUST* play for a consecutive 3:30 time period, or at least one half consecutively of one seven-minute quarter.

WTF!

To say this is alarming demeans alarms.

It is wrong on many fronts. First, all teams have already been chosen and are scrimmaging. The first tournament is next week. Teams would have likely chosen their squads differently. Some teams chose kids based on skill; some teams chose kids based on chemistry; some teams chose kids based on the child's need to simply be part of something, to be with his friends. Surprisingly, coaches are human and recognize this too.

A coach way smarter than I once said, "Being on my team *does* guarantee you PT. However, I define PT not as playing time, but practice time. Being on this team guarantees you the practice time to show me you deserve to play in the game. I am the coach. It is my job to determine all playing time based on our objective to win the game."

The season began on Monday, November 11, per league mandate. Mandating this now, a month into the season, was poor timing at the very least.

In my opinion, PC culture does not have a place in competitive sports. But in our "everyone gets a trophy" suburban world, we don't want to offend anyone, so rules such as this seep into competitive sports. I realize this is a flashpoint issue for many, but I believe it has no place in the game at this level of competition.

I agree it is a nice rule for recreation leagues and some of the lower grades (third grade and below) to ensure everyone gets a chance to play. But, in my opinion, when a child enters fourth grade, they are able to comprehend that not everyone plays equally. (Having coached three sons who have gone through this journey gives me some authority on this topic.)

What this mandate is clearly missing is what it stymies in our young people: grit, grind, and hard work. If I don't play as much as the next kid, I want to work harder to make sure the next game, or next week, or next year, I do. That is called work ethic, being challenged, or the fight within your soul. Don't we want to teach our children this too?

And we were not the only team upset. At a coaches' meeting the next day, other schools were incredulous the league sent this email out after all schools have already chosen their teams. A coach from a team we were to meet in next weekend's tournament raised his hand to speak. He explained he has eleven boys on his team and said, "This means I can't coach basketball until the third quarter." And he's right.

Now, I am certain we all have an opinion of this rule based on the skill level of our own child, and I fully realize I would always rule against something like this. But, for me, I know the rule is insane when my wife, the most level-headed of all of us, said the mandate was ridiculous.

And for the larger teams who have already chosen their squads, what do they do now? Go back to those few boys they chose because a coach knew they just needed to be with their friends, the ones you know may have compromised home lives, trouble in school, a tough time being accepted, the things most parent-coaches are keenly aware of and for which the league never gives us credit.

The powers that be always assume we coaches only care about winning and we are ruining the game. In my opinion the league had given no consideration to the coaches who I know are mostly good people. A meeting with everyone articulating the pros and cons in an open forum prior to the season would have been the most appropriate means of handling this touchy subject—not a directive the week before our first game.

Timing and respecting others' opinions is everything.

This decision was made by a kangaroo court with omnipotent powers in our league and further elucidates why the powers that be are constantly questioned for their authority or lack thereof. And there is no recourse. They are the judge, jury, and executioner on this matter. We simply live with what they dictate.

Horrendous!

WINNING, BUT ...

It was a small, one-day tournament. Just six teams. But a nice, early season gauge of where we all stand. The coach of the host team created the tournament. To no one's surprise, he gave his team the two easiest games. No big deal, I am fairly certain I would have done the same thing given the opportunity to hold a tournament. While everyone wants an easy draw, we all know it is better for the boys to play the best competition week in and week out.

The all-play rule was on everyone's mind, and this was the first test to see how it played out. And it was mandatory. To be honest, it took some of the coaching out of the game. This mandated rule felt dirty.

We created what we thought were two teams of equal talent. We had nine players, so we played a team of five and then a new team of four with Alex staying on to play again. We played our two teams like this for the first two quarters. Each of our two teams played three minutes of the first two six-minute quarters. At halftime, the all-play rule had been satisfied (per league rules) and we could play the final two quarters with the players we chose with no time constraints.

This is not competitive basketball.

We played exactly as our league mandated. Others did not. Whether to circumvent the rule and play their best team for as long as they could or by "mistake," there was rampant abuse. The coach of the eleven player team who spoke up at the coaches' meeting the week before showed up with his six best players. He tried to explain he had a few at a soccer tournament, a few injured, a few on Christmas break, but you could see on his face he wasn't believing the words that were coming out of his own mouth. Instead, he wanted to see where he stood with his six best players.

How do I know I am correct?

Two weeks later, the official league schedule came out, and his school miraculously had two competitive teams and no rec team (the less competitive division). This is how competitive we all are.

We handled the first team at 10:00 a.m. on Saturday morning with relative ease. We pressed from the outset, as we normally do, and we were effective. However, there wasn't the dominance I remembered in our press. Maybe we were just rusty, I thought. We should have beaten the team by forty and ended up winning by twenty-four.

The boys played cocky, and I was not impressed with their defense. We went man-to-man the whole game and did not look particularly dominant. When you play man, it is very vulnerable. You can see who is exposed and who is working at it. There was a lot of exposure.

In sixth grade we threw a variety of zones at people. The boys were more comfortable in a zone and they were good at it. I think I need to listen to my players. I need to listen to the team. I need to listen to what is best for them today.

Coach Roger did not feel we should listen to the boys. He said they would have to play defense at the next level, and they must learn now. He also felt our starting six were better athletes than anyone's starting six, so we should win every defensive battle. After watching this tournament, I did not agree.

Our second game was an hour later against the team who brought six kids (from an eleven-man team). Their six handled our nine for the first half. We were down seven at half—not a position we were usually in.

The second half, we played our starting five for most of the quarter and threw in the new guy, Aaron, for an added spark here and there.

The game came down to the wire and was closer than our seven-point victory. They played great and were well coached. A real team. Backdoor cuts, solid defense, and nailed their open shots. Having only six boys helped them immeasurably. Our AD was at the game. He felt playing our nine on their six made their six tired. He felt the rule helped us gain the victory. I did not feel the same way.

We won, but it felt like a hollow victory to me. As we walked off the floor, a coach from the next game grabbed my arm, smiled at me, and said, "You need to tell your boys the only thing that will beat them this year is their own complacency. You guys have a bullseye on your back. You are everyone's Super Bowl."

I grinned and said, "You are preaching to the choir, brotha. It's exactly what we tell the boys each week."

And he was right. He saw what I saw. Complacency, entitlement, and lack of grit. Shit ingredients for making championship stew.

We now had a three-and-a-half-hour window before our next game. A coach's nightmare. The site was just far enough away from our homes to preclude us from going home and relaxing, but we had no place to decompress at the tournament site. So we all went to lunch together, all twenty-five of us at a local bar/restaurant. We ate lunch, the parents had a few drinks, and I saw the boys tired and scarfing down massive lunches because their fourteen-year-old bodies were hungry: cheeseburgers, fries, onion rings. A recipe for sluggish and sleepy.

So with our lengthy delay, big lunches, and that rule I couldn't complain about any frickin' more, my job as a coach was to get them mentally and physically ready to play even when they were not. I do so with speeches, direction, and shock and awe. By now you know when the boys are ready and when they are not.

We played the host school for the championship of their tournament. The game was tight the whole game. They had nine players, just like we did. They did not substitute like we did. I noticed.

At halftime, I raised my hand, respectfully, and asked to speak to the referees, as I was told by our league to do. They listened, then told me they knew nothing about the rule. (And these were the refs from the company whose owner spoke at our coaches meeting. They had clearly not been informed of the league's mandated rules nor were they interested in enforcing them.)

Awesome.

I then spoke to the athletic director of the host school. He flat out told me I was wrong. He said he was at the same meeting I attended and my interpretation of what I heard was incorrect. We were at odds about two specific parts of the all-play rule: I said you must get the all-play rule out of the way in the first half. Both teams had nine. We needed all nine to get the mandated play out of the way in the first half.

He did not feel this was the rule.

Second, the league head said each boy must play an entire three minute segment or half of the quarter (if not the entire quarter) to qualify as his time played. If he only played a portion of it (less than the entire three minutes, or six minutes of the whole quarter), it would not count toward his 25% all-play time, and thus he must play another entire half of a quarter or three minutes straight.

He did not feel this was the rule either.

When I told him he was wrong, he said, "Don't disrespect me in my own gym." He said it out loud multiple times until my coaches pulled me into our huddle.

Everyone in the gym witnessed our "discussion."

To me, it was clear, we were not all playing by the same rules. Rules that needed both further clarification and, surely, enforcement. If no one was there to enforce the rules, how could they have any teeth? This was gonna be a cluster jam.

In my mind, they knew the rules and were attempting to circumvent them. Of course, what else would I think.

This only added fuel to the fire. This is the school from where Dylan and his parents, one of our school's most insanely vociferous sports families, transferred from back in third grade. They fell in love with our class of boys who were already a talented group of hoopsters. They led the peripheral charge for these boys to play AAU together. They had older twins, and they had clearly already seen the sports landscape of what lay ahead for our boys.

Oh, and they despised their former school. Sure, they still had some friends there, but they wanted to win every time we played and made certain to remind me. And their "friends" back at their old school knew it too.

The second half was a constant back and forth. Our top six players played almost the entire half. It was close, but we pulled out a narrow victory. Dylan and Alex were named to the all-tourney team. They deserved it. There were defensive lapses for both and they missed some shots, but we won the trophy.

My co-coaches said I should apologize to their athletic director. I knew it was the right thing to do. I went up and did so. He looked me in the eye and said he made a call to the league for clarification on the rules I questioned. He said no one answered his call. I could see by the look in that man's eye that he knew he was wrong. I could see it in his eyes.

I went home and I was bothered. We won this small tournament and beat a team we should have, but I knew we hadn't played well, and the lack of clarification about the rule both troubled and ate at me.

I reread the rules given to us at the coaches' meeting. It provided no further clarification. The league head talked us through these rules at the meeting but his words were not on this paper. Then I remembered our varsity rec coach, Tim, was at the same meeting. So I called him for his interpretation and the precise time rules associated with it.

He heard exactly what I heard. I wasn't crazy. That athletic director was wrong. He was wrong but indignant about his correctness even to the point of lashing out at me.

How do you right that wrong?

There is no apology that would help. You chalk it up to life experience.

My son didn't play well. He was one of our long-range shooters and his shot did not fall, at all. We coaches encouraged him to keep shooting. Shooters shoot. He did and it still did not fall. I know it will. Shooters hit shots in streaks. He had one of those days. We all have one of those days here and there whether in sports or in life. It's how you rebound from one of those days that is the mark of a human.

I try to share this with him. He is inconsolable and retreats to the comfort of his iPad. I will get him out in the backyard tomorrow to build back his confidence. He is constantly too much in his head. He needs to become more instinctual. In the last game of the tournament I did not start him in the second half. Another boy was playing better. He knew it and did not complain. He knows. He will bounce back. I know he will.

The victory was ours. The boys earned it and the temporary street cred that came along with it.

I knew I followed the rules. I hated them, but I followed them—and won.

I hated those rules.

17

THIS IS $%#*%^ INDIANA!

After high school, I went to college in the Midwestern town of West Lafayette, Indiana, home of the Purdue Boilermakers. I attended my freshman and half of my sophomore year. It was a long way from home for me, and I was very lonely as an immature, recently-turned-eighteen-year-old away from the only home I had ever known for the first time.

I remember how scared I was when my mom's car pulled away from campus that August day. I had no car. I was eight hundred miles from home. My parents couldn't just jump in the car and visit for the weekend.

And the campus was massive. A sprawling Big Ten university of over 20,000 people, literally like a city dropped out of the sky onto this flat land.

I made some nice friends there but combated my isolation and loneliness with my invisible guardian, basketball. After a few days of trying to figure out how to navigate to classes, I headed straight for the rec gym with my new student ID.

When I walked in, it was as if a choir of angels burst into a multitude of hosannas. It was spectacular. Court after court filled with students as far as the eye could see. I had never seen such a huge facility with so many hoop courts. This place was no joke.

Not bad, I thought.

As I walked deeper and deeper into the gym's labyrinth, I came upon my own personal mecca—the pickup game courts. Eight, maybe ten, courts deep with floor-to-ceiling mesh fabric separators on sliding tracks so balls wouldn't haphazardly fly onto the adjoining court. I had never seen those before. These people, this school, they respected the game so much they paid for those separators—on their pickup courts!

I couldn't even imagine what Mackey Arena (where our school's NCAA team played) would be like, where my massive fellow New Yorker, Jim Rowinski, and his coach with the best comb-over in all of collegiate sports, Gene Keady, ruled the hardwood.

The pickup games at Purdue were competitive. Many of these guys could play. Of course, they weren't good enough to play Big Ten basketball, but they, like me, just loved the game and got the requisite exercise in the process. The thing about basketball is there is not only the typical smell of the musty, dusty, sweaty, smelly gym. There is also something supremely intoxicating about the game: the banging, the physicality, the fouling, and the shit talking. But what struck me differently about these Midwestern games was that it seemed to be more about fundamentals and the love of the game than other places I had, heretofore, played. If you passed, cut, and were open, you got the rock.

These pickup courts were beauty to me. They were comfort. They were safety. They were my old, familiar friend so far away from home.

I walked past one court, then another, then another. Holy crap, Rod Woodson just yoked on a guy (former Purdue All-American safety, now NFL Hall of Famer). Court after court of ten guys and a slew of onlookers awaiting the next game. When I got to the end, I put my bag down, took out my sneakers, and laced up. A ritual that, to this very day, feels almost magical: double socks, ankle supports, Nikes laced tight, but not too tight, just the perfect amount of tightness.

"Can I get next?" I said to a few guys who looked at me like WTF. "Sure," one barely mumbled.

Calling "next" is one of those rituals in pickup games. If you hesitate, you're lost. You just gotta walk up and stake your claim. I have seen too many would-be players pussyfoot around this. If you are offended by the guys on side who came together and probably don't want some rando to screw up their dream team or, if you are the slightest bit shy, you should probably just stay home and play video games.

Pickup's not like that. It works like this: Games are usually played first one to ten. Usually, a guy (or girl) who walks up to a game in session finds those on the side and looks them in the eye and asks, "Who's got next?" or "I got next." Depending on the territoriality of the game, court, or environs, that person will nod or say okay or "We full" or something brutally derogatory and just snicker.

In that instant, you are sussed up. How did you react to their snicker? How were you dressed? Can this guy play? Can he help us win?

Winning in pickup means you get to stay on the court. You win, you stay on. The goal is to have as many successive runs in a row so you get to keep playing. You lose and you sit. If that happens, you immediately try to find the next group and see if they have space on their team. If they don't, you have to wait two games or go to another court to see if you can get another game.

You don't want to be chasing the next game constantly because that means you are not playing basketball. If you came to play ball, losing, waiting, or searching for the next game stinks. You want to run until *you* decide you've had enough.

That is the goal.

When you get a good squad, it can be magic. You keep playing game after game with these guys you just met. It is exhilarating. Then, after proving yourself on a team that has success, the next time you walk into the gym, people start seeking you out to build their very own dream team prior to their next game. To me, this was joy. Far away from home, in the middle of the country, but safe and comforting to me because of the sport I loved.

Basketball was that friend that kept me away from the loneliness and isolation of my current situation. It provided me the comfort, warmth, and familiarity I was so lacking. It's crazy how a sport can do that for you. How it becomes your friend, your social acceptance, your smile away from the loneliness.

Basketball did that for me.

But basketball was also deeper than that too. It taught me to be a student of psychology. To suss out personalities fast. Invariably, there were guys who were all bravado, who talked an endless stream of shit, and who were ball hogs and shot from wherever the hell they wanted, whenever they wanted. I just shut my mouth, pretended to never notice them, and just looked down at my sneakers when they started talkin' their smack to whomever.

I never wanted to be on that guy's team and, intentionally, turned away or grabbed a drink of water from the fountain when he was building his team.

No, out there, at the Purdue University pickup basketball gym, I always wanted the tall, thin, quiet country boys on my team. The ones who had worn sneakers and an old pair of basketball shorts that definitely weren't the latest from Foot Locker, but rather hand-me-downs from three older brothers, and maybe a cousin before them.

Why?

Because this was motherfuckin' Indiana. And if you know anything about basketball, Indiana *IS* basketball.

Even Dr. Naismith, who invented the game in Massachusetts, knew its origins were in Indiana after he witnessed crowds of 15,000 plus at the Indiana State high school basketball tournament in the early days. A unique tournament that, at the time, pitted schools of all sizes against each other for the state title; there were no small and large school divisions, just one big tournament. (That very tournament served as the backdrop for the famous movie *Hoosiers*.)

And until you have played pickup in Indiana, you wouldn't fully understand. I saw it. I witnessed it. I played there and I wanted to be playin' with those cornfed farm boys who respected the game like I did: setting picks, passing, and cutting backdoor, playing D, constant movement, rebounding, and tirelessly running the floor like a pack a wild dawgs.

And them boys could run.

And one thing I could do was run with them. Never fast. Not especially quick, but I had a motor on the court, and I could run for days, never get tired, passed to the open man, was unselfish, filled the lane, and could hit a basic lay-up. You would be surprised how many baskets you could score by just doing those things.

There were a shit-ton of those guys in that gym. And we found each other. We gravitated toward each other, day after day. We would never take each other's phone number or even talk to each other outside of those environs. Nope, wasn't like that. It was unspoken, you just knew when to show up and ball. The times became more regular, the days of the week, the runs became more regular. I swear it helped me become healthier and taught me a quick way to make friends so far away from home.

This game was so simple. Throw a ball into a ten-foot-high basket.

But, for me, the beauty was in how many different ways you could do that or prevent that from happening. It was a test of wills. Your will against another man and how you would fare against each other repeated times down the court. What were you made of on each possession? Did you even care about stopping your man or were you only concerned about taking off down the court and trying to score on your own?

For me, it was a test.

A test, mano a mano, of your will, your desire, your skill set against another man. That's what makes the game so great.

When guys can't cover you, you have broken their will. You have broken them down as a man. They can't stop you. And then it happens again and again, and others start barking at him to step up and stop me. When you blow by him yet again and he commits a hard, egregious foul, he is saying, "I recognize you're are beating my ass into the ground each and every play and that must stop. I recognize that I have to do better for me and for my teammates." This message is usually made violently, willfully, and intentionally to show everyone he means business.

Then it is incumbent upon the man scoring at will to say one of two things in that situation: this guy is a complete psycho and he is gonna hurt me next time I go to the rim, or next time I am gonna blow by his ass yet again and show him who is boss.

Which choice would you make?

My personality was the latter and I have the scars to prove it. That's why I love basketball—and always will.

There were times on the court that I felt so confident that I knew we would beat the opponents even though they looked like better athletes. When you got on a good pickup team at Purdue, there was just an unspoken language. A look. I knew where the ball handler wanted me. He said nothing, just looked me in the eye. I sussed up the guy who was playing him and what my teammate needed from me.

My basic tenet was I knew everything good started from a rock-solid pick from my 6-foot-2, 210-pound (at that time) frame, making profound impact with the point's defender. He knew that too. But it didn't stop there. These guys could play. They saw what I was doing and knew how our defenders would react. All done through a silent language of iris on iris, but really on some other extraterrestrial plane. It's as if I could hear him telling me to roll.

My defender, seeing my pick coming to block his teammate, immediately jumped off of me to stop my dribbling teammate from driving to the hoop. When I hit his defender with a mind-rattling pick and immediately swung my left leg open to roll as I had been taught by numerous smarter basketball minds than my own, his teammate couldn't switch fast enough to get in front of me, and the defender originally covering my dribbling teammate was now behind me in an inferior defensive position.

My dribbling teammate dropped me a perfect dime as I rolled for an easy lay-up and we raced back down the court to play D. No high fives, no slaps on the back, neither of us needed that, just run back to play D.

It wasn't exactly Stockton to Malone or Nash to Stoudemire, but it sure felt like that sometimes.

Behind us, the two defenders now yelling at each other that they've got to cover me.

For me it was that spiritual.

And that's how the games went in West Lafayette. The guys and girls could play and were unselfish. If they saw you could play and would return the favor, all was well. People respected that. People respected the game.

This was Indiana. For those in the know, this was the true birthplace of basketball in the United States.

Indiana is basketball.

18

HOOP DREAMS FOREVER

His father calls. He's not playing.

We all suspected it. He says his son doesn't want to be the lone seventh grader on the team and he needs more time to heal and catch up on his grades after being out of school for a month with pneumonia. He says his son will sync up with an AAU team when he is fully healthy.

I told him I understand.

Brian, the kid with "it," is officially not playing with us. Everyone else had their fun telling me, "I told you so," but I am forever the optimist and want to see the good in every situation.

"It" was not meant to be.

OUR LEAGUE IS composed of four divisions with six teams in each division. There are only five regular season games with everyone playing each team in their division once. There are four weekend tournaments of at least three games each. However, our league has mandated that a team may only enter a maximum of three tournaments so the same team doesn't win every tournament (another PC league rule). Your team's regular season schedule is given greater weight than are their tournament victories, but both are considered in the seedings for the final league tournament at the end of the season.

Our coaches and parents complained vigorously to the league about the all-play rule. Vigorously! For our overzealous questioning, some believe we were given the most difficult division in the league. I agree.

Our first league game of the season is against a weak team. The school from which our new guy, Aaron, transferred. The son of a friend of ours plays on the team. She comes over before the game and gives me a big hug. She warns me they hadn't practiced much over Christmas. I lied and said we hadn't either despite my holding practice every day except New Year's Day.

I want her to feel okay because I know we are about to put a whoopin' on her son's team. Then, I joke, "And then they gave you us for first game, right?" She laughs and speaks out of the side of her mouth, "Yeah, and I told our coach, he better have a frickin' press break ready."

Our reputation precedes us.

We blow them out by 47. And it wasn't that close. Everyone plays a ton. Our league is like that. Sometimes a team of seventh graders must take one on the chin when they have no eighth-grade players at their school. It happens every couple of years. A few bad teams and a few teams that could beat anyone on any given night.

Our next league opponent is one of the other better teams in the league, Northern California Prep School. As I mentioned, they beat us when we were 17–1 and spoiled our perfect season. Therefore, they are in our boys' heads.

Earlier this year, Coach Roger scouted them. He said they were quick and great athletes and they matched up well against us. He talked about how we had never beaten them. I believe we only played them twice—once when I coached, and once when the boys played last season.

I went to watch them in another game. I did not share Coach Roger's fear of this team. I watched them closely and saw some things:

one boy's unwillingness to play defense, patterns of their guard, the way their big men rotated.

I fix a game plan that I think could beat them. I present it to our coaches, and Coach Roger was less than enthusiastic. He feels my defense is too confusing. It's called a diamond and two in which two of our guys cover their two best guys man-to-man, and the other three of our players play a zone. We had used this defense in the past and I think it would work.

I share it with the boys and everyone nods their understanding. There are no questions for the big game the next day.

On game day, I tell the boys we were going to win. The keys to the game are lock down D on their two best players, a physicality that has to be unmatched, and make our lay-ups. If those three things happen, I know we could win.

When the game tips off, it was as if someone dropped the team on Mars with no spacesuits or breathing apparatus. Our team is running around in the wrong positions, guys on their team are totally uncovered, opponents are taking wide open shots. This after a complete understanding of the game plan the previous night at practice.

I may have become slightly unhinged at one of our top dawgs, Dylan. He feels he was playing lock down defense when the coaches and I see he is nowhere near his man. It truly is amazing to see a fourteen-year-old's perception of his play compared to what you are witnessing in the flesh. I say left, he goes right, does not nearly encapsulate the utter disparity.

It is a hard-fought battle, but we prevail by ten. Alex dominates the boards, Dylan scores, and my son, Brock, plays the game of his life, hitting multiple shots, setting others up with assists, and playing serviceable defense. It was a get-the-monkey-off-your-back game because this was the only team to beat us a few seasons back, and many times at this age, the psychological hurdle of beating someone is as great as actually beating them.

The victory is equally important because it is a league victory. Coach Roger, ever the strategist, lets us all know this loud and clear. While he is right, I rarely feel the boys need to know these things because any overthinking in these boys' young minds can tend to spiral into a much larger problem than it needs to be. In my mind, less is more with fourteen-year-old boys.

In terms of the victory, it is a good win. While I may have felt differently two years ago, I hold no aspirations that an eighth-grade team, even ours, could go the entire season undefeated. There is simply too much parity in our league, and any team, including ours, can have a bad day, key injury, or someone not feeling 100% on any given night. There are literally six teams in our league that I think could win it all.

A FIRST FOR OUR SCHOOL

This is the granddaddy of them all. This is the league's largest, oldest, and most prestigious basketball tournament because it is hosted by our local powerhouse high school, Catholic. Our small school has never won this tournament.

In the opening round, we play a team we know we could beat. Our sixth-grade year, we had a few decent battles with them, but they had two solid players transfer out of their school. That left one talented kid, a guard who could fill it from anywhere.

I want to go box-and-one on him (our best defender plays him man-to-man and all the rest of us play zone behind him and get ready to help). Coach Roger insists that was a waste. I listen to him and we go man-to-man.

Just as I predicted, the kid goes off and is hitting bombs from different area codes. I was mad at myself and told myself I was going to go with my game plan moving forward. Coach Quincy agrees with me out of the earshot of Coach Roger. We didn't always see eye-to-eye, and, ultimately, I am the final decision-maker, just as he was in football.

In the end, we blow out the team. I try to give everyone plenty of playing time, especially the boys whom I know wouldn't play in tighter games, which I suspected were coming as we get deeper into the tournament. Apparently, this does not go over well with Dylan. He feels he should be playing more. He feels I played the other starters more than I played him. His parents think he should call me to personally discuss this with me. Which he did, and we did.

I tell him I am concerned that he has been complaining of knee pain when running lines in practice the previous week, that I want some of his teammates to get more time to get better, and that I had heard he was playing in an AAU tournament on the same weekend and that he has already played two games. All things I think he understands.

Dylan is a funny kid. He thinks he does things the coaches don't necessarily see the same way as his mind. He pushes back more than any child and often makes it seem like he is right, and the coaches are wrong—not exactly what any coach wants to deal with, nor what they will tolerate at the next level. This is new. In sixth grade, Dylan was a different kid. Time has changed things.

But Dylan can definitely fill it. He is a point guard in a three body. We try to get him under the basket, and he wants nothing more than to drain threes. And he can hit them too, no doubt, it's just that we are trying to convince him that there is a higher percentage of shots under the hoop and, as one of our tallest players, his rebounding prowess and interior play are much more needed on this team. It is difficult for kids to see their role on a team, how they complement each other, and what their role is.

I simply believe in team above all. I insist on team above all. I will not deviate from that. I don't care about ninth grade. We are in eighth grade, and we are trying to do something no team has been able to do at our school. Ever.

The other problem with Dylan is that he is so damn likable. He is a great kid and hilarious. It's difficult to be too strict with him because he is so funny and charming. When I sit and chat with him alone, we see the court much more clearly. He is a great kid, and he will win a ton of games for us. He already has.

As the second weekend of the tournament approaches, the teams get whittled further and further down and the competition heats up. This is why we play, to test ourselves.

Ironically, we somehow draw Cherryhill in the second round, the same team we pasted in our first league game. And just as I indicated that our perception is we got punished by the league for our pushback on the new rules, we then get an easier draw in the tournament. It is clear the perception is in our own minds only.

We play them on Saturday and destroy them. Our second unit plays almost the entire second half. After the game, the head of the league (the maker of these rules) scolds me for blowing out the first two teams. He tells me we should pass three times before we shoot, only shoot jump shots, and not put it on people.

I look him in the eye and agree. I mean, what do you do? Of course, I agree. I am not gonna tell him he's a jerk and just let the kids play.

Now I have to watch how we win.

On my way out of the gym, a referee from our game sidles up next to me. She indicates she overheard what the head of the league said. She says, "There is no way you do what he said. No way, Coach! This is eighth-grade competitive basketball. The kids gotta learn where they stand now, they gonna learn it soon enough in life."

THANK YOU!

Finally, the voice of reason.

This whole world is getting crazy.

The third game of the tournament is against a team we do not know. I watch them after our game and see they have two players who can play. I draw up a game plan and share it with our team. Stop 0 from shooting threes and make sure 14 doesn't get lay-ups and rebounds. I see it as their two against our five.

At the game the next day, we come out strong. It is a physical game and we are banging. Player 0 is dealing. He is attacking, running around, flying off of picks, shooting, and getting fouled. Our nineteen-point lead is whittled to nine in the third quarter. A nine-point lead against a three-point shooting specialist is nothing. I am scared.

We simply don't seem to have an answer for this kid except to foul him, and he is nine of ten from the charity stripe. The kid can play. My son and Stevie are on fire in the first half, each hitting a number of threes. The second half, they go ice cold. Brock has two points and Stevie doesn't score. That's the crazy thing at this age. The game seems to have a more pronounced ebb and flow.

Ultimately, we stall in the last three minutes and eat up some clock. For some reason, they do not come out and foul us. I don't fully understand this. Why not see if we can make our foul shots, and, if we miss, they get more opportunities to score? For whatever reason, they decide to let us run out the clock and we win by thirteen. I am stunned. I guess you get this sometimes when fathers coach the teams. Perhaps they haven't been in too many close ones. I would have fouled the crap out of us and made us earn it at the foul line.

The difficult and most educational part of the game for me is this: This is now the second time in a week that I have a game plan to stop the team. My game plan is spot on: stop 0 and stop 14. Five on two and I am confident we could win.

The problem with the game plan is that the boys do not execute said game plan. Instead, they go rogue and take every opportunity as a personal challenge to block 0's shot. So, we foul him, and foul him, and foul him. And he makes foul shot, after foul shot, after foul shot. The boys seem to get into a game and forget everything that was taught to them twenty-four hours prior. This is new. This is not the way it used to be. The boys are thinking, or not thinking, differently.

Note for the next game against them: Don't foul 0!

In between games, it is nice to see the parents of the boys from the other teams. Invariably, these are the parents of the boys you have played since childhood in other leagues, or seen at the grocery store, or around town. We are a small community of parents whose boys are all the same age.

I see Babs and wave. She comes over and gives me a hug. I like her. Our sons played AAU together, and her son is playing in the next game. She sits down next to me and tells me about their opponent and how well their team is playing. How her son has gotten so much more aggressive. I smile as I listen, and I could see her speaking more confidently with each breath.

She tells me the team is really coming together and then looks at me and says, "And I think we can beat you too."

Really?

And as if hearing my inaudible thought, she says, "Yeah, I really do. I think we will beat you." And she stares into my eyes.

I just smile for an awkward beat. She guffaws and slaps my arm as I continue to smile but never say what I am truly thinking and the motivation she has now provided me—poster board material to take back to the team to see what they think.

So, I stay to watch the next game. The winner will be our opponent in the championship game the next day, on Martin Luther King holiday. This was a game between Northern California Prep School and Babs's son's team, St. Mary's. We had beat Northern California Prep School a few days earlier and expected them to be in the championship with us. St. Mary's is the team we scrimmaged in our first action of the year, back in November, and, while they hung tough with us for the first two quarters, we blew them out thereafter.

I sit and watch until halftime. And just as I suspected, Northern California Prep School was up 25–12 without their second-best player and their head coach, who was sick. I say goodbye to a few parents and shout some words of encouragement. I go home thinking we are ready for Northern California Prep School part deux just as we expected and wonder if their second-best player will make it back to play tomorrow.

Back at home, Brock and I relax on the couch when I hear his phone ping. He picks it up and his eyes widen: "Dad, St. Mary's beat Northern California Prep School by 8."

"What?"

Then my phone pings. It's Alex's mother. She and I were sitting with Alex and watched until halftime. We both thought we were facing Northern California Prep School the next day. She texts, *You are not gonna believe this. St. Mary's won.* Then I start texting to our coaching staff: *St. Mary's won! St. Mary's won! St. Mary's won!*

We all perceived St. Mary's as a markedly less difficult opponent than Northern California Prep School for the championship of the tournament. We are pumped to put it on Babs.

The next day is difficult. Our game is at 5:30 and the boys do not have school because of the holiday. Waiting the entire day to play the game takes forever. I go to work because I don't want to sit around the house thinking about it. I need something to occupy my day.

My son plays Xbox with his friends, and when I come home around three, he is still in his pajamas. I encourage him to go outside and shoot so he is mentally ready and loose for the game. With fifteen minutes between each game, there is not ample time to get warm.

With Brock, I am always concerned. He does not always seem mentally ready to do battle. He probably wouldn't go outside and shoot on his own unless he was prompted. I prompt him and he goes. I watch him from the window. He has perfect form. The rotation of his ball is perfect. It is an absolutely beautiful shot.

When he feels ready, he comes in and watches another episode of *The Office* before we head off to the championship game. The school is hosting the runner-up game prior to our game. We go watch the third-place game.

Slowly the boys trickle into the gym. Everyone seems really loose.

There is an air of confidence. But, as a coach, you never truly know. Are they really ready? Will they start off slow? Will someone have a horrendous game? Will we be off? Honestly, after all these years coaching, I still do not know what I've got until the end of the first quarter. Until they run. Until they bang. I just never know.

At the end of the third quarter of the previous game, the boys gather their things and begin to walk the same way we went yesterday to the spot behind the benches where we will stretch and strategize. I stop them in their tracks. "Walk this way, I say. We went that way yesterday and I didn't like the way we played."

And here is the deeper level of psychosis I deal with in my own head. I start to believe the same way we walk, the same shirt, shorts, socks, whatever I fixate on, has an impact on how we play. (Ask my team. I have worn the same paint-stained shorts for the last six years, and I think they somehow matter to the outcome of our games.) I am crazy superstitious. And it is usually not if we have a good game and blow people out. It is generally when we play poorly.

Last night, I thought we played poorly. We still won, but we played poorly. So, I change some things, like walking a different way around the gym. When we walked to the right, we won two games by more than forty points. When we went left, we only won by thirteen. We are going right tonight.

And then the game starts and they score the first five. In the past, I would have started screaming. My two co-coaches have told me to sit back and relax a little and let the boys play before screaming at them. It is sound advice. They are correct.

As I gnaw at the inside of my cheek, we start to score bucket after bucket. Brock drains the first of his threes and we are off to the races. It all starts with defense. Defense is the key to every one of our games. Tim locks down their best dribbler, and Aaron provides length and backup in doing the same. These two boys will always be able to play anywhere. They can play D.

But no matter how well they play D, all everyone cares about is O. How many touches I get, how many points I can score, how many claps from the crowd. A tough lesson to learn for all players.

I take the time to explain the game of basketball very simply to the boys. Two seven-minute quarters of running time. There are only a finite number of times you can run down the court on a fast break or set up an offense. We have played many games and we can score between forty-five and seventy points pretty regularly. We better make sure our opponent scores less. The only way to do that is to play killer D. This year, we have generally held teams under thirty. That's darn good. That will get it done most nights.

And it does tonight. We run St. Mary's off the court and beat them by twenty-seven. We win the Catholic tournament for the first time in our school's history. A first we will have forever. My son makes four of six threes that night and doesn't play most of the second half. He is awesome. Our big guy, Alex, and Brock have a special connection on the court. They are the best pick-and-roll combo in the league. It is beautiful to watch.

Brock, Alex, and Stevie make the all-tournament team. I feel Tim should have for his defense. He is the best defender in the league and should have made the all-tournament team because of it. Kids care about these things. They want the hoodie that says, "All Tourney."

I was very proud of my son. Not for his selection on the team, but for his play. Less than thirty days ago, I didn't start him with our first team because he wasn't playing well, and now he was among the best players on the court. It all changed in one month's time. Things change at this age; something just clicks. I remember holding back tears when he hit his third three of the second quarter. He's come a long way.

It was gratifying to win a prestigious tournament in our league and be the first at our school to do so. As such, our team will always be remembered for that—if people remember such feats.

For me, I will have the memories and the folklore. I will remember.

But now, halfway through the season, I also notice things are different on the court. By eighth grade most kids have played some type of club or AAU basketball. Dribbling out of the press is much more commonplace. Kids of this age don't get as rattled as they used to in fifth and sixth grade when they are pressed. Most have matured and are used to the full court pressure from AAU.

While watching the games last year, I noticed that no teams pressed. I wondered why and even questioned it. But now I see. Kids are just better now. And our boys see that too. They aren't as dominant on their press as they used to be. It is alarming. We have to change. And we are. We didn't press once in the tournament. Not once. We are 9–0 and maybe that's just not who we are anymore. Maybe we aren't as dominant as we once were. Or maybe we have evolved.

KOBE

Kobe Bryant, his daughter, and a few other parents, players, coaches, and the pilot died in a helicopter crash today. They were on their way to their daughters' basketball game. There was dense fog and the helicopter crashed into a mountainside in Calabasas.

Kobe was going to coach his thirteen-year-old daughter's basketball team.

My son is thirteen.

This was particularly close to home not because of Kobe's many accolades on the court, but rather because, now, at this stage in his life, he was simply a father who wanted to be with his daughter and enjoy the game they both loved.

Coach Roger, Coach Quincy, and I are just dads who want to be with our sons, enjoying a game we all love. That's all we've ever wanted.

My heart hurts. My heart hurts for all the victims of the tragedy who, from what I understand, were all doing what they love.

My eldest son was born in Los Angeles and together we claimed the Lakers as our own because of Hud's birthplace. Kobe's exploits on the hardwood were legendary, but he was, ultimately, just a dad like many of us.

Rest in peace, my brother. We, and many others just like us, for the rest of eternity, shall carry on the legacy of being with our children for you.

We are one. Together. Hoop dreams.

19

NOT TAKING THE HINT

So you've probably read this far and thought this guy must be a straight-up baller, right?

Yeah, not so much.

The reality is, I wasn't even good enough to walk on to my Division III Brandeis University varsity basketball team. I played on the JV team for less than six months. I transferred from Purdue in the middle of my sophomore year, and then Brandeis coach and former Celtic great, Bob Brannum, gave me a look-see. He was a massive man, with hands that looked like catcher's mitts. He had me come to a few varsity practices where I saw, firsthand, I wasn't so special. A slow, 6-foot-2 guard who really couldn't hit an open jumper.

Dang!

And coming from those pickup games at Purdue, I thought I could play.

They let me play JV. I had fun, and it was a great way for a transfer student to meet a few great guys, but JV basketball lost its luster quickly.

And that would have been a fitting end to a wonderful career for most. But, oddly enough, that is not where my basketball story ends. You see, I never gave up basketball.

From that point forward in my life, a time when most would have seen the abundantly clear and concise handwriting on the wall, basketball became an even greater passion of mine.

That's when you know it's love. When you fail at something and keep coming back to it. Like the girlfriend you know isn't right for you because she's out of your league, but you keep hangin' on just so you can be seen with her.

No, from that point on, there was an almost constant and maniacal search to find a game: a town rec league with former high school heroes, pickup games at 91st Street and Columbus Avenue after a night of drinking with the boys, or a law school traveling league around southern Vermont and New Hampshire in the dead of winter when most humans were comfortably sitting fireside because the roads were too treacherous.

You see, hoops was in me.

And the strange thing is this. I got better as I got older, like way better. I found a long-range jumper, and I would score twenty and thirty a night in some of these leagues. I truly got that good. I ultimately became the player I wanted to be … at thirty-four years of age. You know it by the way others play with you. It's a feeling.

And if you ever got in the zone when shooting, it became otherworldly—an out-of-body feeling really. The zone is when you know the ball is going in before you even release it. Like whatever shit you throw up, from wherever, in whatever position, it's going in. It's as if you are one with the bottom of the net, operating on some higher cosmic plane. These times don't often happen for mere mortals or maybe come more infrequently for others, but when it happens, it is a feeling like few others on this earth.

For those few fleeting moments, in some small, insignificant way, you can imagine what it felt like to be Bird or Iverson or MJ or Curry, but instead of being in The Garden, The Forum, or The Palace, you're in your own tiny subculture of hoop-dome, in some random, shitty, poorly lit gym somewhere on the globe.

But that didn't matter.

For me, that feeling was like no other. And the competition, the mano a mano, no refs, calling your own fouls, which you would never call because you weren't a big pussy, were the primary accelerants to that fire. When you were beating someone's ass so often, play after play, that he had no choice but to foul you as hard as they could to let you know he gave up.

He knew it. And I knew it.

And I frickin' loved that feeling. And I think that is why so many men never want to give that up. That desire to legally bang and test yourself against another man in a physical activity at something you love, it's just ... it's ... it's nirvana.

While most people would have given up after a college experience like mine, the love of the game just continued to fuel the invisible guardian that was inside of me.

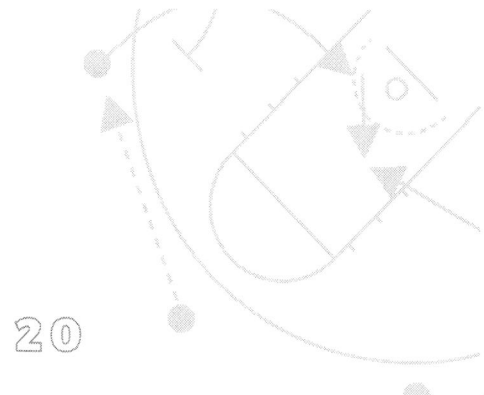

20

SMOOTH LIKE SANDPAPER

It has been two weeks to the day since winning the Catholic Classic. The day after we won that tournament, the boys left on a class trip to Sequoia National Park with their classmates. It was a nice respite for all of us.

As a coach, of course, you worry about everyone getting rusty, the lack of reps, and forgetting the small details. But this is eighth-grade parochial school basketball, and we are preparing the whole child for the world. A week in a national park with their teachers and classmates learning about the great outdoors is invaluable for a child.

Then there's the flu. A couple of kids had to come home from the trip, and soon it spreads through the school like a minor plague. And there's nothing you can do about it. Mix in a few sleepovers, a few play dates, and it spreads further. I got it and was laid out for three days. Then, my wife got it and was down for another four, like totally out. When Mom goes down, the house starts to crater, a human sinkhole really. We try everything to get her better, but the flu simply needs to run its course.

Various boys are on the edge. A few no-shows to practice and I pray it doesn't get worse. Now, we are thanking ourselves for the break in the schedule. We need the time to get healthy as a team. We practice Tuesday and Thursday of the following week with a skeleton crew. Then, AAU tryouts and interviews for incoming freshman (our eighth graders) at the local high school and you start to understand what takes priority in everyone's lives. Finally, Coach Quincy's dad makes an unexpected visit to the hospital, and it is easy to see how eighth-grade basketball practice becomes the lowest priority.

I understand. I have to. These are the things you can't fight. There are much more important things to everyone. Perspective. And with the Super Bowl featuring the local favorite San Francisco 49ers, you can't expect kids to want to practice on a Sunday. We have officially taken a backseat to life.

It is now the Monday after the Super Bowl in early February. We have our first game in a few weeks on Wednesday, and the Christian Sisters tournament (our area's other private high school) the following weekend. This would begin the final push to the end of the season; another nine games and it is all over, our four months ... and a lifetime.

And then it came.

It was just an email. An email in the middle of my workday from our athletic director. Five of my boys are academically ineligible due to grades—more than half our team. This comes as a huge surprise for many reasons. All these boys are good students. And, more importantly, the semester is not even a week old. The boys took finals, went away for a week, and had only been back for a week of school.

How could they all be academically ineligible after a week of school?

And it was one class. A torrent of phone calls and a deluge of emails from parents flood the school's office. Finally, our headmaster has to step in. The questioning gets so bad, the teacher who placed these boys on probation wrote a scathing email to the entire eighth-grade class saying, in sum, the parents and their disregard for teachers was the reason he was leaving the teaching profession—to get into marriage counseling!

Now, as many parents inserted their jokes about our "challenging parents" versus what this teacher might encounter counseling married couples, I tried to understand what the ramifications of academic ineligibility at our school actually meant.

In sum, it is merely a warning that their grades, at this current time, are below 70%. As such, they would be given an opportunity to bring their grades back to at least 70% by Friday or face a week off in which they could not play school athletics. The main point of contention for most parents is with only a week of school under their belts, these students should not have had to endure this kind of grade check so early in the semester.

And I know this teacher to be a good man. He is a principled man. He is doing what he was supposed to do according to the letter and spirit of his school's policy. He has been a teacher here long enough. He does not baby the students but rather holds them to a higher standard, trusts that they are growing up, and wants to play a role in helping them along the way. I truly believe that.

As a coach, of course, I want my boys to be eligible. But as Coach Quincy reminds me, as these boys mature and grow into young men, these are the valuable teaching moments that help them build character, grit, and resiliency. All the things we want our children to possess.

And to their credit, our school holds steadfast in their policy. There are calls to the headmaster to point out the flaws in the way the policy was written. The school analyzes their policy and acknowledges some of its inherent flaws. Ultimately, however, the school decides, even with the flaws as written, the policy is clear. It was a first-class cluster jam with both sides being partially correct.

I AM NERVOUS about this game all week. St. Paul is always an aggressive team, and they have one of the best, if erratic, players in the league. A kid who looks way older than his eighth-grade year and can go to the rack as strong, and hard, as any player in our league.

At this point, we have not played a basketball game in two weeks, which is an eternity in youth basketball. Sure, we had practiced a few times and got in some intrasquad games, but it's not the same. The true game experience is not something you can replicate in practice, no matter how hard you try. Any coach will tell you that.

We jump out to an early lead and build it to a thirteen-point halftime lead. It feels good, but it is also unnerving. The second half starts, and we begin to collapse. There were a string of missed lay-ups and they put together a nice run. This happens in every game of basketball and, as a coach, the key is to know when to call a time-out to stop the bleeding.

I call a time-out. The boys look flat. I try to tell them to dig in on defense and collapse on the scorer. He wants to do it all himself. Anyone can see that. And, although we are in a man-to-man defense, it is vital to sag off our individual men to help our two best defenders, Aaron and Tim, who are guarding him man-up. It is simply man-to-man with a zone mentality.

This is a difficult concept for some, but, in our league, you generally have two kids who can score. If our guys can lay off their man and double and triple team the guy who doesn't want to give up the ball, two things happen: one, we get a lot of hats on the ball, and, two, we frustrate the scorer.

A frustrated scorer is good because he starts to force things. He knows he doesn't have the teammates to help him win this game, and we know that too. Usually, he will start to force shots to prove to everyone he can win the game on his own. His frustration then generally carries over onto the defensive side of the ball. There, he makes it his own personal mission to block everything at the rim, which causes him to pick up a few silly, overly aggressive fouls.

And it plays out exactly like that.

We stop their run, start making a few buckets, and frustrate the kid to the point where he picks up his fourth foul by the end of the third quarter. Our lacrosse player, James, again plays the game of his life and even challenges their scorer when he takes a fast break with their scorer running even with James the entire way. With the hoop nearing, James goes up for the lay-up and leans into their scorer to draw a foul. The kid backs off to make sure he doesn't pick up his fifth foul. James then has the presence of mind, and body control, to make the lay-up. An unbelievably savvy play from a kid who plays the least amount of basketball on our team.

We withstand their rally and end up winning by twenty. But it didn't feel like twenty. It was a hollow victory. We didn't play well. One of our dads counted. We missed fifteen lay-ups. It felt like thirty from the sidelines. As a coach who goes over lay-ups and fundamentals day after day after day in practice, this is what induces the grand mal.

The victory was ours. But there is a cloud. The cloud of uncertainty that looms. What are the chances all five boys can play in the tournament coming up this weekend? Will we have to forfeit? Which boys will be eligible? How many players will we have?

Before the boys leave, we huddle in a tiny alcove of our gym as teams warm up for the next game. I am coming down off the postgame high and quickly deconstruct the game. I tell a few kids what they did wrong and a few others what they did right. I tell Dylan he can't be a ball hog and we must distribute the ball and Tim that he needs to convert his lay-ups. The compliments follow. The coaches tell me it's time to leave and we disperse.

A half hour later Dylan's dad emails me with his son's stats, indicating among other things, Dylan was six of twelve shooting and how is that selfish. He asks me to call him, which of course I do. When I call, he asks me if I called his son a ball hog in front of the other boys. I say yes and he leans into me reminding me of the positive coaching alliance class I took. Essentially, saying I am denigrating his son and will never do that again or I will be reported.

I apologize.

I realize this has been a rough week for all of us. I explain we all talk like that with one another and always have. We try to motivate each child in their own unique way. I said it in the heat of the moment, right after the game and, as such, it is on me. Of course, he never heard the compliments his son was given nor was he privy to the other coaches telling me for the past two weeks that all the other boys are getting tired of Dylan's selfish play. And he shouldn't. This is our team and we need to handle those things internally.

In my mind, the parent is always right. He knows I am not an evil man, and I know he is out to protect his son at all costs. This family is doing everything they can to make certain Dylan plays at the next level. Their older boy always made the teams at Catholic but rarely played. Dylan is their last shot. It is vital to them.

After the phone call, I still feel bad. I drive to their home to apologize in person. When I get there, father and son are not home because Dylan is now practicing with his AAU team thirty minutes north of us. We just had a game and he is traveling north to play on another team. We talked with all our players at the beginning of the year about holding off on playing AAU until after the season. We wanted to do something special that had never been done at our school. We felt everyone needed to be at full strength and rested to win it all. I was ignored.

It's too much. I know this is too much for this boy.

I sit and talk to Dylan's mom. She is very receptive and appreciates my visit. She explains their sensitivity to being called a ball hog. Apparently, a few years back, the leading scorer on their older son's high school team was called a ball hog by the coach in front of his teammates and then lost the team. She explains they might have some PTSD from it.

Either way, I know they are right. I am embarrassed that I said it. In fact, I am often embarrassed what I say to these boys. Usually they fire back with some wild quip or rib me too. It's just the relationship we have by now. But I am guilty. I am guilty of being too comfortable with these boys.

It is my fault. I own it and even apologize to Dylan in front of his teammates at next practice. But I am quick to reiterate that, more than anything, I love each and every one of them and would never mean anything in a negative manner. It is clearly my problem. I need to check myself.

THE NEXT DAY is picture day at our school. All the school's teams gather in their basketball uniforms for that iconic, lasting photo that will freeze us in time for all of eternity. That photo we will go back to periodically over our lifetimes to remember the kids of our youth. Most likely they will not be kids we stay in touch with over a lifetime, but they will hold these cherished moments of a bygone day and time when we ruled a small space in our corner of the world.

And I, much older than these young men, will hold this photo much closer to my heart. I am older, I have lived more. I know how special these moments are now. These boys won't realize that until days gone by.

No, I will remember these faces with reverence and joy for what they meant to me and my son and our unabashed togetherness for all these years. No, this photo means way more to me.

And then the first shoe drops.

As we are lining up for pictures, our dean of students marches into the gym and tells our AD that Dylan will not be eligible for this weekend, not because of the class with the four other boys, but because of another class. We gather to smile for the photo, but we know there will be fireworks tomorrow. We know there will be more, and we know various parents will be bringing a whipsaw of heat upon the administration.

But the next day, one by one, we get word from each parent that their boy made it; they raised their grades above 70%. The other four, somehow, all qualify for our tournament.

We all gather for pizza and watch films in the school's computer lab, prepping for the tournament the next day. Coach Roger pulls me aside. He has an app that analyzes the game and spits back the data. Dylan was 6 of 22 from the field in the previous game, not 6 for 12 like his father said in the email. I smiled. We both knew.

We watch film of St. Peter's, the team we believe we will play the next day, a team we already beat in an earlier tournament. We believe St. Peter's would win the first game tomorrow because these two teams met last week and St. Peter's won. We plan, diagram, and make each boy abundantly clear of their responsibilities. We have pizza to keep it relaxed. Everyone understands the game plan. We are prepped and ready.

Dylan is there but he is angry. He feels his social studies teacher, Coach Applewhite, who coached these boys in seventh grade, would not help him get a passing grade and, thus, enable him to play in the tournament this upcoming weekend. According to Dylan, he is a point short. He feels Coach Applewhite is sticking it to him so our team would go into the tournament weaker and have less of a chance of winning.

I do not believe this. I am not a conspiracy theorist. Again, a principled man simply doing his job.

As we leave, I inform Dylan we got approval from the league for him to sit on the bench and support his brothers. Dylan says he will be there. Coach Roger witnesses the entire conversation.

The next morning, Coach Quincy and I head down to the tournament to watch the first-round game, the winner of which we will play that afternoon. Coach Roger has taken his daughter on a college recruiting visit and will not be able to attend.

It is close the entire game. St. Peter's hits a shot with under thirty seconds left to put them ahead by one. But, miraculously, the other team, St. Claude, wins at the buzzer—the team for whom we did not prepare.

Why would it go as planned?

Luckily, I had seen the victorious team a few weeks back at another tournament and took some notes. (My wife called me a loser for going to watch that game by myself.) We will quickly switch the boys' focus to our new opponent. St. Claude's has a big, agile center who beats people down the court for lay-ups and slashes to the rim relentlessly. I know we need to stop him in order for us to win.

A few hours later, we can't stop the big, agile center who beats people down the court for lay-ups and slashes to the rim relentlessly, but we still win. We were without Dylan and we still won. The other boys picked up the slack. It wasn't pretty, but we won. But to our dismay, Dylan never showed up to support his team.

There are some rumblings from the other families about Dylan not being on our bench to support his teammates. I avoid the controversy. As a brilliantly intuitive mind (ha!), I am starting to see how his father's lashing out at me, Dylan's suspension, and his absence from our game may be all interconnected. But we have more games ahead of us, and I don't wish to start a whole 'nother war in the middle of this tournament. I know what I told Dylan. I know I had told him to be there. Coach Roger heard me tell him. I know why they weren't here.

And ironically (or not), the next game we play is Dylan's old school, St. Thomas' Sanctuary. I had never lost to this team. A source of great pride to both of Dylan's parents and me. And again, Dylan is a no show. Coach Quincy and I are not surprised. It was another close game, but we wore them down and came out victorious. Alex led the way with scoring and Stevie, James, Aaron, and Tim did the rest.

My son was hurt and couldn't find his groove. It was now the third game in a row of Brock's disappearance. As good as he was in the Catholic tournament and now this. I was frustrated, but he was genuinely hurt with multiple thigh injuries, and his brothers picked up the slack. It felt good to win both games without Dylan. He was among the leading scorers on our team, but, now, there was some more pronounced fracturing among his teammates. To a boy, they indicated to us that Dylan wasn't passing when they were open; both co-coaches backed them up. I saw it too.

I rationalized; this happens as the boys age. The divisions start to happen. Kids get better and are taught and motivated by other coaches, trainers, and their parents and, next year in high school, it gets really real.

I am a softie. I hate this. Most families now have their own agenda, their own wants and desires for their son. It is painful to witness. Painful, especially after all these years together. To know what we have all been through together and then this? It makes you question your fellow man, or at least those people you thought were friends. People change, they become way more competitive. They feel they have to, to look out for number one. There are a finite number of spots on the freshman team next year.

I still hold no grand illusions that my son will play in high school. I push, try to motivate, but I simply don't see that burning desire in him, and, ultimately, I am fine with that. Some parents are not. Brock is a good kid who loves his friends, and I don't want him to change from that.

After a first-round bye (because we won the Catholic tournament) and winning these two games, we are slated for the championship game on Sunday against our archrivals Northern California Prep School. We beat them a few weeks back in our regular season game. In this game, we come out flat and never really recover. There are no outside shots falling, and they stuff the middle better than they had the first game against us. We end up losing by eight, but it doesn't feel that close.

I know we miss Dylan.

For all the heat he gets, I love the way Dylan plays because he gets to the rim. Sure, he forces it sometimes, and sure he will fight through an ill-advised triple team now and again, but I believe you need guys like this on a team. I think those types of guys can have the reins put on them once in a while and relearn how to get everyone involved.

But with Dylan, it was funny because for all our previous years together, he was never *that* guy. Up until our sixth-grade year, he occupied the middle of our press and was an amazing leader of that tourniquet with his length. It was only somewhere in his seventh-grade year that his shot started to fall. There were games I would go to that year that he scored twelve or fourteen points on jumpers alone. Now, it was never game after game, but he could fill it now and again.

Then in our summer league, we saw that he could flat-out score. He had a deadly jumper and was probably one of the leading scorers in summer league. His evolution from vital role player to leading scorer had just recently happened over the last year and a half. And it has been fun to witness. Shocking for the other boys to see, but fun as a coach to see his improvement, due in no small part to his parents' finding the best trainers and leagues for him to play in. They are behind all this. And the credit goes to them—and Dylan's hard work.

The problem is there is a price to be paid for all that hard work. The boys are not calling him to join them on their video game matches or to go bowling or to hang out and sleep over. Things have now changed. It is difficult to witness from my vantage point. I unrealistically wanted them to stay together forever.

But forever is a long time.

We got home after the championship game loss and I got a call from Dylan's dad. I didn't answer it. I was upset. I figured he wanted to explain why Dylan wasn't there. I didn't want to hear the excuses.

The next day Dylan's mother called and made an excuse why they didn't have Dylan come. It did not feel genuine. Later in the conversation, she admitted they were embarrassed to have to explain why Dylan couldn't play. It was very telling. I know all their friends from their former school were there and this family neglected to face the music. All of us coaches were unified and on the same page; all of our families were behind the team.

I try to be prudent in my criticism of families. Sure, I want to run the table and go undefeated. That is what I strive for our team every year. That is the expectation I have for myself, even as a dad-coach. I hold myself to that high regard. I know it may not be attainable, but that is what I am trying for.

I never thought a child would become academically ineligible for an eighth-grade tournament. But it turns out it happens. I just wish I was fully armed for that tournament. If I lost with my whole team there, it's on me. Handicapped without it, still on me, but you dream the what-if scenario over and over in your head.

The damage done to our team could not be measured. I wasn't sure how the boys felt about their teammate not being there. I suspect they didn't think much of it. I wanted Dylan there to show his brothers' support. That is the way we have always operated. I guess things have changed that now. Things are different. It hurt us all as coaches because we thought that is what we have always taught—the brotherhood. The sticking together when times get rough. The digging even deeper when our backs were against the wall.

Did Dylan's lack of attendance erode what we had taken all these years to build? Be selfless, play D, and rely on the brother next to you—the basic tenets of our team.

In practice that week, we give everyone an open forum to talk about anything they want to. No one spoke. They are fourteen-year-old boys.

The Monday after the tournament, I get another email indicating three more boys were potentially academically ineligible for this week too. They have until Friday to get their grades right.

Un-frickin-real.

And to make matters even more conspiratorial, they are all in the history class taught by their seventh grade basketball coach.

Dylan gets reinstated for the next game and I don't bench him. Coach Roger and Coach Quincy did not agree with me; they felt I sent the wrong message to the team. I know they are right. I just didn't want even more drama and I know Dylan needs the reps. I also always had a soft spot for Dylan. Yet now he is an outsider on this close-knit group of boys, and I feel all this was more his parents' doing than Dylan himself. I don't want him to further recess into depression.

I soon learn my actions have broader implications.

THE BLOW OUT—AND NOT THE GAME

Our second to last league game is against St. Mary's, the team we scrimmaged and beat in the finals of the Catholic tournament. They are a solid team, better than when we played them a few weeks back.

Again, we don't play well from the start. We have always been a slow-starting team, usually taking a half to get things rolling. But now I am certain the all-play rule has compounded that.

We were up 25–21 at half and surprised to be that close. At the start of the second half, we tried a new press, a 1 x 3 x 1. We had practiced it a few times the week before. We had purposefully gone away from our press after the first tournament in December because the boys no longer felt comfortable with it. People were breaking it and we lost confidence.

Coach Roger is not happy with me. He feels we are the coaches and, as such, we should be the ones dictating what the boys do. He feels the boys are lazy because it is difficult to press when most kids have now become better dribblers. He is right, but my coaching philosophy is simply different from his.

I take the opposite tactic with the boys. I want to listen to their words and craft scenarios in which they are comfortable and in which they feel they would excel. I agree with Coach Roger that with certain teams on certain courts, our press could again be effective, so I institute it against St. Mary's because I feel St. Mary's might struggle with it. They have one good dribbler who would do everything. If we stop him, we will have a reasonable chance of success.

So, we press. And it is successful.

There are times when you press for different reasons. Sometimes you are trying to get turnovers, sometimes you are just trying to show pressure, and other times you want to tire the opponents out by constant in-your-face D.

We tire out our opponents. Sure, they break the press a number of times, but that's what pressing will do. If you are afraid of giving up easy buckets now and again, you should never press. Pressing is not for the faint of heart. But you have to be all in when you commit to it. The real catch is seeing how long you can stomach staying with it. That is where the coaching comes in. Are your guys getting tired? Are their guys getting tired? Who is winning most of the battles down the court? When those victories are in your favor, you stay with the press at all costs.

And we do and ride the game to a seventeen-point victory. A seventeen-point victory that feels like winning by four. That is the type of anxiety I regularly feel.

The most unfortunate part of the game happens in the third quarter. Dylan has the ball, tries to dribble through three defenders, and turns the ball over. Stevie, our point guard and Coach Roger's son, and then Alex, our center, scream "pass the ball" out loud on the court.

Dylan hears it and is clearly hurt by his teammates calling him out. My co-coaches tell me to get Dylan off the court, but I elect to keep Dylan in. Again, I feel pulling him out in that instance will embarrass him further. I tell everyone to calm down and let them finish out the quarter.

I have coached these boys a long time. I had never seen that before. I had never seen them go after one another like that. My co-coaches indicated how frustrated all of the other boys were and how it was now coming to a head. I contributed to this by not benching Dylan after he didn't show up at our tournament. It was me. Both of my co-coaches would have disciplined Dylan. I elected not to. Because of that election, I had now affected the rest of the team. It was coming to a head as we headed into the final push of the season, our last home game and the PAL tournament.

Perfect timing.

To complicate matters, we have a school winter break next week and some families want to go away for a few days. I want to practice to get ready for the tournament the following week. Again, this is where life gets in the way. Everybody is all in and gung-ho when it is perfectly convenient for them, but the minute they want to go away, they run for the hills, regardless of the intentions of the basketball team. Again, it is eighth-grade hoops.

I know I need to relax, but that shit drives me crazy.

The last game of the season is destined to be anticlimactic. It is against the worst team in the league. They have four players to start the game. We sit one of our guys to make it a little more even. A fifth player of theirs shows up halfway through the first quarter. We play with five from that point on. By the end of the third quarter we have seventy and they have eight.

The best part of the night is totally unexpected. Our team is in the gym forty-five minutes before the game for our shoot around, a time when the boys just take shots on their own and stay loose. Our rationale is that we want the boys to have shot fifty to a hundred times before they enter the game that evening. In a basic pregame warmup, they might be lucky to get off twenty. It is important to get plenty of shots up before you ever enter the game so you are already warm.

As we warm up, I see a small African American kid from their team sitting on the sidelines watching our players. It was as if he was watching a Leviathan rising from the depths of the ocean about to engulf him in its jaws. He is watching our boys in awe.

I see him a couple of times and finally go over and say, "Hey, we have a whole buncha extra balls. You can start shooting if you want?"

He says, "Okay, thank you."

"I am Coach Meyer," I tell him.

"Yeah, I know. You coached me in summer league in second grade. I know Tim and Brock and Stevie."

I could not place his face all these years later.

No way. Yeah.

I say, "Well, it's nice to see you again."

He says, "You too."

The boys remember him. And he starts to come into focus for me.

After we played, I was walking out of the gym and there was a middle-aged white dude waiting for me. You know the kind of guy you can see from a mile away. He was standing by the exit clearly waiting for me and we met eyes.

He said, "Hey, Coach."

I said, "Hi."

He saw I didn't recognize him. "I am Chris's dad."

Now it rang the bell. This man was the father of the boy I met before the game.

I said, "I remember you." I told him how Chris introduced himself to me before the game.

He told me how much fun Chris had that one summer playing with the boys. It's all he talked about. I could see from the dad's eyes that he meant it. He continued that the summer with our team was so very special for his son and how much his son enjoyed my coaching. That made me feel good. He thanked me and complimented me on our team. I told him how much I appreciated his kind words. How much it meant to me.

I walked out of the gym that evening never thinking once more about the victory. All I could think about was bringing joy to Chris's summer that one year. For some reason, that made my day so much better. That's why I coach. That right there, a memory of someone else five years removed from the event and the joy my son and his teammates brought to another child's life. That was what it is all about.

Sometimes the insanity of the competition and trying to win clouds these moments that truly matter. It's nice to be brought back to earth once in a while.

21

...AND A CHILD
SHALL LEAD THEM

The games on Saturday and Sunday started at 7:00 a.m. at the El Rodeo School in Beverly Hills on the corner of Whittier and Wilshire across from The Beverly Hilton. Between fifteen and thirty guys regularly played each week. Some the same, a few stragglers, sometimes friends of friends.

Even when the powers that be decided to padlock the school gate to prevent us from playing (I assume a liability issue), we grown men would climb the metal fence to play our game. These men were eye doctors, dentists, actors, contractors, screenwriters, ex-cons, agents, heroin addicts, and movie producers—even some movie producers who were heroin addicts.

It was a great run.

For two hours a week, I could put my screenwriting frustration behind me and forget about life for a while. I would play both days. My wife (my girlfriend at the time) would sleep in, and I would bring her a Peach Pleasure Jamba Juice or decaf vanilla latte from the Coffee, Bean, and Tea Leaf on Sunset where I saw everyone from Renée

Zellweger to Dave and Chad from the Chili Peppers to the Double Mint triplets from the Wrigley's gum commercial. Those were some fine-looking triplets!

My best friend at this time of my life was a man who was fifteen years my senior. He was 130 pounds dripping wet, played with a baseball cap on backward, and could absolutely shoot the frickin' lights out. It happens sometimes. You play pickup with the same people weekend after weekend, twice a weekend, and, somehow, you form this unspoken partnership. This kismet. It's kind of like dating. You just find someone you like having on your team.

For Mike and me it was the classic post and guard combo that just worked. I would flash to the high post, he would deliver me the ball, I would spin and square to the basket, either drive to the hoop, or, if his guy would sink to double on me, dish to him on the wing for a wide open jay.

And here's what made it so great: We were both unselfish. It didn't matter who scored. Never did. Neither one of us could care less. We simply wanted to win that game so we could play as many consecutive games in a row to get a good sweat in. That was our trophy. You lost and you had to sit for at least a game, maybe two when it got crowded. That is not why you got up early on a Saturday and Sunday. You wanted to be in that first game of the day and not lose.

When Mike and I played, it was like a ballet. He knew exactly where to go on the court, and I would deliver him the ball as he would step into a perfect jump shot or I would make a motion with my eye and he would throw a pass near the rim as I spun off my man for an alley-oop. It was as perfect as a plié in both form and substance.

It wasn't until after we had played together for a number of years that I found out he was the famous music producer of my youth; he produced music for people like Shaun Cassidy, Leif Garrett, the Osmonds, and Donny and Marie. What in god's name are the chances of that?

I remember reading my brother's *Tiger Beat* magazine as a child and seeing the perfectly coiffed middle part of Shaun and Leif and watching *The Osmonds* and *Donny and Marie* variety shows with my grandparents on Saturday nights. Now I was playing hoops with their music producer on some random basketball court in Beverly Hills. It just seems too fantastic to believe.

We had such amazing weekends together, and although a change in venue has kept us apart, I think of him often with reverence and joy in my heart, mind, and memories. A great friend during those struggling times of writing early in my career, and a fitting culmination to my playing days.

AND A NEW BEGINNING?

My career ended in the most glorious way possible at thirty-nine. Not a torn ACL. Not a popped Achilles. No heart attack on the court.

Nope.

My career ended with the birth of my son Hud. Our first child.

He was born and I never again felt that same gravitational pull, that bloodlust, that hunger I had, heretofore, always felt about playing basketball. It was as if my subconscious told me, "How could you waste any time away from this newborn beauty?" And, as God as my witness, I never even gave it a second thought.

That light, that inexorable blinding light of the first thirty-nine years of my life, just, poof, turned off like you would flip a light switch on your wall, when I saw my son's face. It was as if some internal ticking clock just went off inside of my being. Maybe it was the greater cosmos saying that I had played more basketball than most normal men of my age, or maybe it was because I was another year older, but I just never wanted to go back again, nor did I ever go back again.

My biggest regret is that I phantom-ed on all my El Rodeo hoop buddies.

172 • FOUR MONTHS ... AND A LIFETIME

My wife would always ask, "Don't you want to go play ball with the guys anymore?" She couldn't believe it either. It had become such a regular part of our lives since we had met that she was shocked I never wanted to go.

I guess it was just my time. From the day of our son's birth, I felt this internal change in me. During my whole life up to that very moment, it had never been difficult for me to break away and play. Now, I didn't even want to leave the house to be away from my newborn for even one minute. He was just so beautiful, and cute, and ... mine.

Looking back on it now I can see it was simply my complete and utter joy of being a dad. A father to this beautiful blue-eyed little man. I would get up and lift him out of his crib, take him upstairs, and just start playing with him. It's all I wanted to do. This hangin' with my newborn son was my new basketball. It was a time of maturing (yes, albeit very late in life, I realize), and I never hesitated, not even one moment, because I wanted to be with our new family—the one my wife and I had created.

My son did that for me. He helped me grow up.

As it turns out, his birth was the official beginning of my transition in life from playing basketball to living my joy of basketball through my sons. It was as clear as day. Kinda like a *Hoops Lion King*, the circle of basketball life. I tapped out of my playing days with the birth of my first son and soon thereafter started thinking about when he was going to be old enough to start playing in our local rec league.

I found out it started in kindergarten. I had four years to prepare.

And that is how my coaching career began.

I had played a lot of competitive basketball with a ton of great men and women over the years, but once I hung them up, I didn't miss it. I have the memories. They still come to me in my dreams at night or in seeing a game on TV or just reminiscing with friends about the glory days: a sick pass I threw, a night I couldn't miss, how much fun I had with a group of guys who similarly loved what I believe is the greatest sport on earth. From the Nerf in my room, to my hoop on Hillview, from middle to high school and Duke to Purdue, it was always magic to me, and brought a smile to my face and joy to my heart. A joy that will never be extinguished.

Basketball did that for me more than anything else. It let me be a competitive athlete much longer than I should have. I was grateful. I am grateful to the game, and I still treat the game with the reverence and respect I believe it deserves.

Only now I am a coach.

22

A BOX OF CHOCOLATES

This tournament operates like March Madness: lose and you go home.

The tournament runs over the course of six days, Monday through Sunday. The seeding for the tournament comes out the Saturday before the tournament begins. In the past, the head of the Parochial Athletic League or PAL has invited the coaches from the four division winners to meet with him and discuss the proper seedings. This is where the jockeying for positions generally starts.

I had the pleasure of going to one of these a few years back, and it was an absolute debacle. All coaches, myself included, had ulterior motives of why they/we should be seeded where. The tournament director listens and makes suggestions, but no one is ever happy. It turns into a gerrymandering crap fest.

The league director gets it right this year. He invites no one and takes it upon himself to build the tournament. He is capable. As long as he doesn't simply take each division winner and make them the top seed, I think he will be fine. Our division is loaded with better teams than most divisions. This is good for us because it tests you during the regular season. In some of the other divisions, only the first-place team is solid. I believe this will benefit us in the end—at least I hope it will.

Ideally, you want to be the top seed and play the number four seed if all of the seedings go the way they are supposed to, which they never do. In our case, there are two equally good teams, St. Maximilian Kolbe and Northern California Prep School, whom we would prefer to have to play each other as the two and three seeds in the semifinals. That would align us with the four seed for the semifinals. I think this is the way it will match up.

I can't explain being 14–1 and feeling like we are 8–8. I guess the hunger, seeing the imperfections, never being satisfied is, what, healthy? I make certain we tell the boys how proud we are of them for going 14–1 in the regular season and winning two of the three tournaments they were in and being in every final. That is saying something.

But, in the end, we are all chasing the 'ship. Without the 'ship, this all means nothing.

My speech to the boys at practice today is simple: "I need every one of you to find something extra. That one extra thing that will take you to another level, to take us as a team to another level. We all need to find that extra gear and ratchet up our game. That is what it will take. That is what it will take to win a championship."

The boys look at me. They make eye contact with me. They actually seem like they are listening. These thirteen- and fourteen-year-old boys actually seem like they are listening.

Maybe we have something here. Maybe I finally got through.

We wait with anticipation to receive the email. We expect it sometime in the afternoon.

As I wait, I think this is it. I will only have potentially four more games with these boys, maybe fewer. Nine years of being together of their fourteen years. How utterly astounding. What an absolute privilege. What an amazing feat for a coach, his son, and some friends. How could this be? How could we be coming to an end?

It seems like just yesterday that we rolled out the ball in kindergarten and they couldn't even reach the rim. Now they are draining threes from twenty feet. A blink of an eye. A dream. A kaleidoscopic dream vision of the best sort. Living the life of a dad with his son playing a game we both love and to share it with a couple other dads and eight other families. So fantastic. So perfect.

But my heart starts to hurt.

My heart starts to hurt because of the foreboding onslaught of clouds I see in the distance. The clouds that will bring the inevitable rain, that will wash away all that we had and that will eventually bring the sunlight of a new day and new coaches and new journeys in each of these boys' lives—without me. And I without them.

I will retreat to the comfort of my third son and his friends and try to reignite the flame with a new group of boys, whom I already love and whom I already have been coaching since kindergarten. My co-coaches say I am the lucky one. I have another son. They both have only one son and got to live this journey once.

I have lived it three times.

And they are right. I am the lucky one. My God, I am the lucky one.

But I can't dwell on this now. I have a tournament to win. I have some boys to coach. I have more joy around the corner.

We will practice Sunday morning, our last time before the tournament starts. We are ready. We are geeked up. The boys are ready. The schedule is Monday, Wednesday, Friday, and Sunday. Lose one and we are out. Win or go home. The first two games are at a small gym. We may press. We may press hard.

The seedings come out by 2:00 p.m. In reality, it couldn't have been more perfect. The seedings were done intelligently, taking into account a totality of the season. I think many of us were surprised. It was the correct formula to use. And as such, we were given a very winnable road to the finals. Three wins and we will be in the championship game on Sunday. One at a time, but three winnable games, no matter which teams beat which.

It is now up to the boys.

We hold a practice on Saturday night from 7:30 p.m. to 9—the only time gym space was available to us at our school. Having practiced Thursday and Friday, this may have been a mistake by me to try to get another practice in and then schedule another one for Sunday morning. At some point it becomes information overload, and the boys disengage.

That is certainly the case Saturday night. They are tired. It is late. And it is the worst practice of the year. My co-coaches had other plans, so being alone didn't help matters.

To compound things, my son says he reinjured his leg. It frustrates me. I want all of us to be at full strength for the tournament. I think the simple things like hydrating your body, eating properly, and washing your hands are the practices we try to reinforce so the boys have a fighting chance to be at full strength. I clearly care way more than any of these boys do. And that's the problem.

As I gather the boys for our huddle at the end of practice, I tell them it was their worst practice. They know. They had been fooling around, cutting up, and not taking things seriously. Again, my fault for trying to get one more practice in before our first game.

Sometimes, it is better to just leave things alone.

I decide to give them Sunday off completely and reconvene at our first game Monday evening. We are the number one seed, and we are playing the sixteenth seed in our sixteen-team tournament. We played them the first game of the year and won 46–15. It is not a difficult choice to let them have the day off, their last day of winter break. Next week they will be back at school and have to contend with homework, grades, and a regular schedule again.

And we're ready. We truly are ready. Coach Roger and Coach Quincy are so much better than I at seeing the full picture. Especially Coach Roger with all his football coaching experience. He knows the value of a day off. This is good. This will be good. Let the boys relax and not think about basketball for a few hours.

On Monday, it begins. Sixteen teams trying to win it all. In one week it will all be over.

IRONICALLY, WE PLAY the first game of the tournament at 5:00 p.m. on Monday. The boys look relaxed. I play the boys equally and let them run. I ask them to concentrate on their man-to-man defense, pass, and have fun. After a slow start, they relax and steamroll to a 72–18 victory. The concentration is on passing and being unselfish. All the boys play their part and sometimes even make one too many passes. It's a mistake you are okay with.

I am crazier than most, so I stay and watch two more games to see who we would play on Wednesday and another game in which I had interest. As it turns out, we will play St. Paul on Wednesday evening, a team we beat in the regular season, but a team who also has one of the best players in the league.

Our goal will be to attack him, get in his headspace, and try to lure him into early foul trouble, exactly what the opposing team was doing to him this evening. In fact, he had four fouls by the second quarter and sat most of the second and the entire third quarter. But somehow his teammates held on and, when he finally came back in the fourth, he won the game for them.

The kid is a baller.

The final game that evening is a huge upset. The fourth seeded team in our division upset the fourth seed in the tournament. It was a fabulous game, back and forth, and ends on a blocked shot at the rim at the buzzer. The first three games of this tournament are all won by teams in our division. I always thought our division was the toughest.

Tuesday we practice after school and discuss the game plan. The boys understand their roles completely. Tim locks down the best player, 35. Aaron shuts down 33 and prevents him from taking any triples. The rest clog the middle and focus on 35 and make driving difficult so Tim can stay out on him and prevent the triple. Our thinking was this would frustrate the kid and force him to want to do more than he should.

I am nervous about the game. Nervous because now I don't want any one of them to be our last. I know it is coming either way by Sunday—just not today, Lord. Just not today.

The game starts and they come out in a zone with 35 sitting in the back middle of it; we know his coach's decision to protect him.

We get up by a few. Then a few more, until it is 16–5 by the end of the first quarter. Tim has hit a few bombs and is playing insane defense on the guy; Aaron is locking down 33. The game plan is working. They make a little run in the second quarter, but we withstand it and get up by 28–12 at half. Sixteen points never felt so small.

The second half we step on their throats outscoring them 24–6. Tim, Aaron, and James have locked down their two leading scorers, so much so you can see both of their boys quit by the end of the third.

It feels good. On offense the boys come together. Dylan leads the way, Tim and Brock bump five threes between them, and Alex does his normal thing. We have a lot of guys who can score so it is difficult to know who to scheme to stop.

THE SEMIFINALS ARE set. The top four seeds all make it: us playing St. Bede the Venerable and Northern California Prep School playing St. Maximilian Kolbe. The tournament director nailed it. He got the seedings correct. See, he didn't need the coaches' input after all.

Thursday practice before the game is a combination of film and on-court mapping to show how we will attack their defense and play defense on their best player, the best player in the league. The boys are bored. They want to run. Of course, we coaches don't want to run to risk anyone getting hurt twenty-four hours before the game. My son is battling his thigh injuries. Coach Roger suggests a quick cryogenic treatment at a walk-in facility in town that evening. We get home and my son is more concerned about his history exam.

This is who Brock is.

By this point in our life together I want him to say, "Dad, you are the best. Let's run down there right now and get me healthy so I can rip it tomorrow night." But that is my inner voice. That is what I would have said to my father. That is what I would have wanted.

But Brock is not me. If my life with my sons has taught me anything, it is that we are all individuals. And being individuals makes this life so much more interesting in the long run. It took me a long time to figure that out. Children have a way of making that abundantly clear, like a sledgehammer to the medulla clear.

We ice his legs and schedule the appointment for the next day after school. That night, he soaks in an Epsom salt bath, and we rub down his thighs with medicated gel and wrap them, just as we have done the entire week.

When I wake the next morning, he is on our couch moaning. His throat hurts. We take his temperature and he has a 100.76 fever. He is staying home from school. Now I am thinking I am losing my best long-range shooter for tonight's game. I give him meds and head to work.

To me this is the irony of all ironies. We start playing a game we both love and build this epic journey together, my son and me. We get where we always wanted to be together and it ends like this. The same thing happened in the football season and sometimes I think it's the pressure of it all, of the big moment. Have I created this anxiety in him that causes his body to shut down? Or is it just the luck of the draw? Just life's way of reminding us that things never line up perfectly for you.

I am not sure we will ever know. I think I have been conscious of all this to try to keep a relaxed, comfortable atmosphere, but maybe I am the problem.

We take him to the doctor. Actually, we take him to the cryogenic lab first to get a treatment on both his thighs. He says he feels better. I know, an eighth-grade athlete at a cryo lab? See, I am no better. I am part of this whole problem.

When the doctor returns, she tells us there is no strep throat. What a relief. But he tests positive for the flu. He is highly contagious and will be for the next four days. He could take the whole team down. We order Tamiflu and pray we got it early enough, holding out hope of a miraculous recovery.

Then, our school's athletic director calls. He and I are good friends. He tells me the dean of students just visited him and says Brock is not eligible for tonight's semifinal game because he did not attend school today. It is the final reality. As much as I want my son on the court with me, the handwriting is abundantly clear in boldface, 72-point font sized print. My son has perhaps played his last game at his school.

I am devastated. I am crestfallen. I am hurt for him, for us, for the team. Brock made us better. We could win without him, but Brock made us better.

I need to be strong.

I need to be strong for my other boys—for the team. They can't see me hurting or upset. Confidence. I need to show extreme confidence in the face of this disappointment and adversity.

Another irony about this entire situation is this:

My wife and I have been married for nineteen years. Anyone will tell you, she is clearly the better half of our marriage: kind, calm, prudent, thoughtful, and intelligent. The best partner in life anyone could ever wish for. When she hears the school called me and told me our son could not play, she is pissed. Like, legit pissed. She went through the school handbook, the sports handbook, everything she could read, and found what she believes is a loophole.

Now I try to calm her down (when our entire life has been the other way around). But, at the base of my soul, I am beaming with pride. This woman has got some piss and vinegar that I have never seen before. The school told her, her baby can't play, and mama bear no likeee!

When we finally talk reasonably, I explain it may be better coming from her to address the dean of students about Brock's availability for the championship game on Sunday, if we are lucky enough to win this evening. She agrees.

When she picks up my youngest from a class trip, she sees the dean of students preoccupied but attentive. Angie goes in for the strike and to get clarification about Brock's availability for Sunday. Somehow, she gets approval "if he is healthy."

Not sure I would have gotten that so quickly. Angie heard what she heard and didn't push for too much more clarification. She got in her car and left.

We have an option. There is a glimmer of hope.

THE BASKETBALL LIFE

It is not how we wanted it to go. It is not how the book should end. We are supposed to win in glorious fashion on a last-second shot made by the unsuspecting boy at the end of the bench. Ya know, the movie version.

Yeah, that's not how it ended.

It was odd. It was odd leaving my house without my son. For all those years, for all those games, for all those practices, it was he and me, us, together, entering the car and talking, talking about hoops, about life, about silly things, or nothing at all. It was just us. Our time. The few minutes before the pageantry started, or we picked up a few other players on our way to a game or practice.

That was what was weird about today. He wasn't with me. I was alone. He was home, on the couch, sweating the fever out that the doctor said would take a few days, four days of highly contagious time.

What are the chances? What are the chances of spending a lifetime with your son and his friends to end like this, at less than full strength going into a semifinal game at 16–1 and the number one seed?

That is life.

That is the way life works.

That is the greatest lesson in all this.

You wanna make God laugh? Tell him your plans.

We come out slow against St. Bede the Venerable as we always do, and miss a litany of easy buckets, foul shots, and get killed on the boards. Again, we have a clear and concise plan that we had gone over, showed on film, and articulated on the court during various practices and walk-throughs. That plan was not executed.

For whatever reason, the lights, the pressure, the gym filled with cheering people, whatever, there are times the boys go out there and just do not execute what we draw up. And of course, there are times we coaches do not iterate fast enough, and we do not place them in positions for success fast enough to make up for that disconnect.

Ultimately, it is all my fault.

I am the head coach of the boys varsity comp team at St. Matthews Day School. The buck stops with me. I didn't get it done—again.

My phone pings like crazy after the game from well-wishers aplenty. I am grateful for all the kindness and warmth.

I pull into my garage and see the door open.

My ten-year-old son sticks his head out: "I'm sorry, Daddy." Just the word *Daddy* makes me feel like a million bucks.

"Thank you, Mack."

He gives me a big, long hug with a full embrace. I can feel the warmth of my son. Then he releases me and looks into my eyes with the brightest, widest smile on the face of this earth and says, "But we got my game tomorrow and we're gonna win that and then go to the championship at Golden 1."

And time stops ...

I literally see time stop as I am standing there in front of my ten-year-old, like a pause in the motion of living, a freeze frame in life.

My son keeps talking with his wide toothy grin but I hear no audible sounds.

And I see ... this ... this is my life.

I am a coach. I am a dad. Daddy.

This is my life.

One door closes and another one opens again.

I have three sons. It has been the same with each. We've won, we've lost, and life goes on. It continues. And in the small spaces in between are the moments. The moments I have always treasured and never taken for granted. The silly things at practice, the smiles, the improvement, the ribbing, the laughter, the heartache.

This is my life. The basketball life. And I love it.

As I write this, my time is not over. Mack has a lot of basketball left in him before high school.

I know I am the lucky one. I am so the lucky one.

After my smile and embrace with Mack, I walk over to Brock on the couch. I gingerly ask him if he is upset.

"Well, I wasn't there, Dad." And goes right back to his iPad.

Again, life.

Again, my son. Forever level-headed and pragmatic like his mother when his father is the emotional basket case. Yin and yang really do work in this world.

The thanks come in. And true to form, Stanley, Nicholas's dad, writes a heartfelt, kind, thankful letter to us all. He gets it. Always has. He's busy. He's out in the world making money as one of his industry's top execs. You can see he loves what he's doing and is having fun. But I see a part of him that may be a little different than most.

He wants to be us coaches, but he can't. He is relied upon by thousands to make money. He is an executive. But I know he came from humble means and loved and played basketball his whole life. He told me stories of taking his son into the driveway and schooling him at basketball, like we all did to our sons to show them our stuff. This year, Nick finally beat him. For the first time.

Like me, when I was fourteen, beating my older brother on 41 Hillview Drive in Pleasantville, New York, on that hot summer day.

And it's happening the world over every day.

You finally beat your father

You finally beat your older brother.

You beat the friend you previously never could.

It's happening each and every day.

It's happening each and every day on courts all over the world.

It's so simple. All you need is a ball and a basket. Just a ball and a basket.

23

FOREVERMORE

How do I say goodbye?

How do I say goodbye to a group like this? Boys who have been my son's friends for all these years through thick and thin? Boys who have shared the glorious memories we have all shared in life from five to fourteen years old? While nine years of life is merely a blink of an eye in the grand scheme of things, I have been part of these boys' lives for a lifetime really, their lifetime thus far.

And I am nine years older myself. You realize that at my age. No one can buy more time. It's the most precious commodity in the world.

I will never say goodbye. I can't. I won't. These boys have become such a profound part of the fabric of my life that I will never leave them. Maybe we will never share what we had again: the practices, the games, the joking around, the ribbing before and after. True. It was special, beyond special. Life-altering really. The best I could have ever hoped for.

It was exactly what I wanted: to be with my son and his friends as they grew up. So many practices. So many games. So many weekends and weeknights. So much time. Nine years of playing together.

Hundreds of games. I did it. I did it with a smile on. I did it willingly. I did it with joy in my heart, even when it was difficult to do so. I have absolutely no regrets. I have hoarded all the memories that will last my lifetime.

And, boys, I promise you I will never leave. I will simply never leave you. Any of you. You will all move on to high school, college, and beyond. You will all grow up to be fine young men, choose a spouse, and start your own families. You will, that is the circle of life for all of us, for all of humanity. That I could play an infinitesimally small part in your lives for these few years is for what I will be forever grateful.

These were simply the times of my life.

See, my true joy is not, nor has it ever been, to travel on some fantastic trip to some remote port of call or ancient landmark and see with my own eyes the things normal people marvel at or wish to see and experience once in their lifetime. For me, my true joy, what makes me tick are the small interpersonal moments of eye connection I have experienced with all of you. When I can see you are truly listening to what I am saying, learning, and I can tell by your smile that you know your coach genuinely cares about you, wants you to get better, and has pride in what you have become. *You* are my joy. Every one of you. *You* are my fantastic trip.

I have heard so many people tell me how much they admire all the time I have given to all of you, to all of my sons and their friends. Your parents, grandparents, aunts and uncles, and family friends have all been overly complimentary and generous with their kind words. To a boy, your families have impacted me with kindness aplenty.

But what they do not seem to realize is that I receive a thousand-fold of what I give. You boys have provided me with so much unparalleled joy, so much fun, so much laughter, so much wisdom, so many happy moments and memories—my lord, the amount of fun we have had together. I simply cannot say it enough.

And what you have taught me …

The lessons you have taught me about myself, my life, and grit, and people, and ... and ... love. I cannot say it enough: I love you, boys. I always will.

A dream childhood with friends who shared the same love and a coach who fell more in love with a game, again, through his son and their friends.

And I will die.

One day, I will die as we all will. But when I die, please never feel even one inch of sadness for me because I will have a smile on my face. No, I will have a big-ass grin on my face because I have lived and loved the lives of my sons and their friends in a way few men ever will.

I know my experience is unique. I am so eternally grateful to our school for allowing me to coach my sons. I pray the tradition continues. And hopefully, along the way, I taught a few children the absolutely magnificent game of basketball.

What a game.

You all have bright futures. Very bright. There will be ups and downs along each of your roads. It happens to everyone. Everyone! No one gets out of this life without being tested. Tested by people, situations, predicaments. Tested by life. You will have those tests. And when those happen, of course all of you have great and able parents and families. But I will also be there. If you need me, I will be there too. For advice, a helping hand, or just someone to talk to you. I will be there. My home is always open.

I will always be your coach, but now I become your greatest cheerleader.

I love you all. I always will.

Now go frickin' crush life!

EPILOGUE

This is a story of my middle son, Brock, and his friends. You got that.

What I never mentioned to you is that my son is deaf in one ear, has been since birth. Not a big deal, you say, he has another ear, in which to hear.

True dat.

The doctors told us he shouldn't play contact sports. There is the risk of a hard fall and jostling something in his other ear, potentially rendering him deaf. How do you tell a child not to play a sport he loves when every sport involves some level of contact? A rough foul, a colli-sion of heads diving for a loose ball—it could happen at any moment. Life is random that way.

But, you see, Brock's partial deafness has never defined him. He wears a hearing aid at school, not in sports, and not at home. He doesn't want to. He has innately learned little tricks (the tilting of his ear to those who are speaking) to get by. And I am not in his head. I do not know what he does and what he doesn't hear. I just know it does not define who he is, never has, and I suspect it never will.

Why tell you about this? Why tell you of my son's "handicap" now after all this?

Because we all have handicaps of one sort or another. Just don't let them define you.

My kid's a frickin' rock star. And the world needs more rock stars.

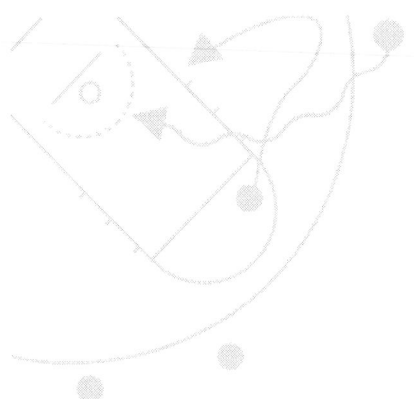

RULES OF
THE GAME

1. We want the child to have fun.
2. We want to show them hard work, structure, and a process for success (like how the assembly line to make a hamburger works at In-N-Out Burger).
3. In a process, there is always the opportunity to change and make better if you see something to improve upon—innovate!
4. We want to show them teamwork—how people with different skill sets can work together to achieve a unified goal.
5. Competition—testing yourself mentally, physically, and emotionally.
6. There is, and will always be, someone bigger, faster, stronger, smarter, whatever. Just do you and know who you are.
7. Resiliency—how to fight through the difficulty and get up; always get up and come back for more.
8. Winning with dignity—you have been, and will be again, on the losing side. Remember how it feels. Empathy.
9. Enjoy your teammates and coaches and build memories. These are the times of our lives.
10. It is, ultimately, just a game. See Rule 1.

FAVORITE
BASKETBALL MOVIES

Hoop Dreams (documentary)
Hoosiers
The Street Stops Here (documentary)
Rebound: The Legend of Earl "The Goat" Manigault
The Pistol: The Birth of a Legend
He Got Game
White Men Can't Jump
Fast Break

ACKNOWLEDGMENTS

I would like to thank—

My best friend, John Webb. I am not certain I can fully express how much your love and friendship mean to me. You inspire me every single day of my life. Every day!

Brenda Perrota, my high school English teacher. You showed me the love of words and awoke the sleeping giant within. Thank you for believing in me when I didn't believe in myself.

Professor John Rubadeau, the greatest English teacher a freshman could ever have. Scared the tar out of me and the words into me. You are why I write.

Professor Thomas Ohlgren, another man who made medieval English fun to read. You rock!

Professor Alice Kelikian. I hope Brandeis realizes what they have in you. You saw me for just who I was—and still liked me.

My editor, Sandra Wendel. You are nails. No bullshit. Terse. To the point. Decisive. Just nails!

Domini Dragoone. Your talent is sublime. I know one day you will be too big for me, but remember me when …

My agent, Angela. They will soon all see what I see in you and your talents. To infinity and beyond!

My sound engineer from Post Audio, David Whitaker, for taking a chance on a new author with a crazy vision.

Mom, for giving me the greatest childhood I could ever dream of and always believing. Always.

Dad, for your love, counsel, and friendship forever and ever more. Thank you.

My brother Craig, thank you for playing with me all those years … all those years.

My brother Cary, what a time we had just … playing. To be back there one more time … heaven!

My wife … everlasting … simply the best. You make me better every day.

My boys … for showing me what true love means. All I want is you.

John and Chris. We did it. We got to coach our sons. How utterly fantastic! We will always have the memories.

And, finally, to Humanity. Chill the %$#* out and do good for your fellow Man and Mother Earth. We got this together!

ABOUT THE AUTHOR

Chris Meyer currently operates a few tech companies. Most recently, he built funandmoving.com, the world's largest exercise and rehab platform for people just starting out or recovering from an injury.

Prior to his career in the tech industry, he wrote, directed, and produced a low-budget film called *Black is White*. The feature length race relations drama was written up in *Variety* as the film to watch from the Independent Feature Film Market in New York City. It was one of twelve international films chosen for the Rome Film Festival. When the film wasn't chosen for Sundance, Chris loaded up his car and moved to Hollywood to become a screenwriter. He made a living as a production assistant working for Herb Ritts, the premier fashion photographer of his time, and on various studio lots.

Chris grew up in Pleasantville, New York. He has a Juris Doctorate and Master's in environmental law (Magna Cum Laude) from Vermont Law School and a BA in politics and history from Brandeis University. He has been a licensed New York State attorney for over twenty-eight years.

He now lives in Northern California with his wife of twenty years and their three sons. You will, most likely, find him on a field, or in a gym, coaching one of his sons' teams.

And, like his Opa before him, Chris simply believes in family above all.

Made in the USA
Columbia, SC
14 July 2021